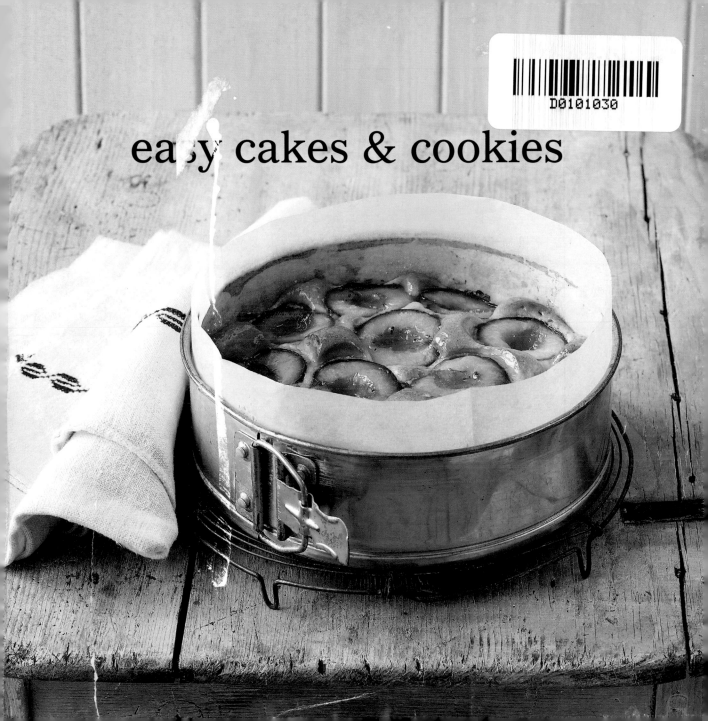

easy cakes & cookies

easy cakes & cookies

cupcakes, brownies, muffins, loaves & more

RYLAND
PETERS
& SMALL

LONDON NEW YORK

Senior Designer Toni Kay
Editor Rebecca Woods
Picture Research Emily Westlake
Production Gary Hayes
Art Director Leslie Harrington
Editorial Director Julia Charles

Indexer Hilary Bird

First published in 2012
by Ryland Peters & Small
20–21 Jockey's Fields
London WC1R 4BW
and
519 Broadway, 5th Floor
New York NY 10012

www.rylandpeters.com

Text © Susannah Blake, Claire Burnet,
Maxine Clark, Linda Collister, Ross Dobson,
Tonia George, Brian Glover, Hannah Miles,
Miisa Mink, Isidora Popovic, Sarah Randell,
Annie Rigg, Laura Washburn and Ryland
Peters & Small 2012

Design and commissioned photographs
© Ryland Peters & Small 2012

UK ISBN: 978-1-84975-211-4
10 9 8 7 6 5 4 3 2 1

US ISBN: 978-1-84975-212-1
10 9 8 7 6 5 4 3 2 1

A CIP record for this book is available from
the British Library.

US Library of Congress Cataloging-in-
Publication data has been applied for.

Printed and bound in China

Notes:
• All spoon measurements are level, unless
otherwise specified.
• Ovens should be preheated to the
specified temperature. Recipes in this book
were tested using a regular oven. If using a
fan-assisted oven, follow the manufacturer's
instructions for adjusting temperatures.
• All eggs are medium, unless otherwise
specified. Recipes containing raw or
partially cooked egg should not be served
to the very young, very old, anyone with a
compromised immune system or pregnant
women.

Contents

Introduction

Baking is one of the most deeply satisfying activities – and can be almost as rewarding as the final result of your labours. When it is a dreary day outside, there is nothing like taking refuge in a warm, cosy kitchen and surrounding yourself with the delicious aromas of freshly-baked treats. And then comes the enjoyment of sitting down, whether with friends or family or simply a good book, and digging into a sumptuous slice of cake or a melt-in-the-mouth brownie fresh from the oven with your cup of tea.

For baking inspiration, *Easy Cakes and Cookies* is all you need. Including a huge selection of some of the best baking recipes, there is a recipe to suit every occasion. As an after-school snack, Cupcakes and Muffins will put a smile on the kids' faces, while Breads, Buns and Scones will provide a traditional accompaniment to an afternoon tea. Look to the Large Cakes chapter for an impressive birthday cake, or for a decadent dessert try one of the Tarts, Pies and Cheesecakes.

As well as the convenience of being able to quickly whip up a delicious treat from a few basic ingredients, another advantage of baking your own treats is the knowledge that those ingredients – the freshest free-range eggs, real butter, good quality vanilla extract – are likely to be of far superior quality to anything bought in the supermarket. You will quickly learn that no cake can taste as good as the one you bake yourself. Whether you are an experienced baker or an enthusiastic beginner, there is guaranteed to be a recipe here that will delight.

Cupcakes and Muffins

Warm chocolate muffins

275 g/2 cups plus 2 tablespoons plain/all-purpose flour

30 g/3 tablespoons unsweetened cocoa powder

2½ teaspoons baking powder

½ teaspoon bicarbonate of soda/baking soda

185 g/6 oz. dark/bittersweet chocolate, very roughly chopped

100 g/3½ oz. milk chocolate, grated

2 large eggs, beaten

100 g/½ cup light muscovado/ light brown soft sugar

300 ml/1¼ cups sour cream

100 g/7 tablespoons unsalted butter, melted

a 12-hole muffin tin/pan lined with paper cases

Makes 12 muffins

Make these muffins to eat straight out of the oven whilst the chocolate is still soft and melting – there won't be any left by the end of the day! You could make them using milk instead of sour cream, but the sponge won't be as soft and crumbly.

Preheat the oven to 200°C (400°F) Gas 6.

Sift the flour, cocoa, baking powder and bicarbonate of soda/baking soda into a large bowl and stir in the chopped and grated chocolates. In a separate bowl, beat together the eggs, sugar, sour cream and melted butter. Add the liquid mixture to the dry ingredients and stir until just combined and the mixture is fairly stiff. Don't over-mix otherwise the muffins will be tough. Spoon the mixture into the muffin cases to fill almost to the tops.

Bake in the preheated oven for 20 minutes until risen and firm. Leave in the tin/pan for about 15 minutes before turning out as the mixture is quite tender: cakes made with sour cream or buttermilk have a lovely tender crumb. Turn out onto a wire rack and serve warm or cool.

Toffee pear muffins

150 g/1¼ sticks butter

150 ml/⅔ cup milk

3 large eggs

6 tablespoons dulce de leche

100 g/½ cup light brown soft sugar, plus extra for sprinkling

300 g/2⅔ cups self-raising flour

1 generous teaspoon baking powder

2 rounded teaspoons mixed/apple pie spice

2 large, ripe but firm pears, cored, peeled and chopped into small pieces

1 rounded tablespoon porridge oats

a 12-hole muffin tin/pan, lined with paper cases

Makes 12 muffins

The toffee in these muffins is dulce de leche: thick, luscious Argentinian caramel, sold in tins or jars. It also makes a delicious sauce to serve with sautéed pears, apples or bananas, for a quick dessert, if you have some left over.

Preheat the oven to 200°C (400°F) Gas 6.

Melt the butter in a small pan and leave to cool slightly.

In a large mixing bowl and using a balloon whisk, whisk together the milk, eggs, 2 tablespoons of the dulce de leche, the sugar and the melted butter.

Sift in the flour, baking powder and mixed spice and whisk together. Scatter the chopped pear over the top and, using a large metal spoon, gently fold it in until just combined.

Divide the mixture (which will be quite sloppy) between the muffin cases. Sprinkle each muffin with a little extra sugar and a few porridge oats. Bake the muffins in the preheated oven for 30–35 minutes, or until risen and lightly golden.

Leave the muffins to cool for 10 minutes or so, then, using a small, sharp knife, cut a small cross in the top of each muffin and spoon half a teaspoonful of dulce de leche into each one. Leave it to settle, then add another half a teaspoonful to sit on top. Eat while still warm.

Sugary jam doughnut muffins

75 g/⅓ cup sunflower oil

150 g/⅔ cup plain yogurt

½ teaspoon vanilla extract

2 large eggs, beaten

275 g/2 cups plus 2 tablespoons self-raising flour

½ teaspoon bicarbonate of soda/baking soda

a pinch of salt

100 g/½ cup caster/granulated sugar

75 g/⅓ cup blueberry jam

Topping

25 g/2 tablespoons unsalted butter, melted

50 g/⅓ cup caster/granulated sugar

a 6-hole muffin tin/pan, lined with paper cases

Makes 6 muffins

This is a recipe for anyone who likes a warm sugary doughnut but dislikes the deep frying involved in making them. Of course the result is more cakey than bready but they are every bit as delicious, as they ooze jam and cover your lips with sugar crystals.

Preheat the oven to 190°C (375°F) Gas 5.

Put the oil, yogurt, vanilla extract and eggs in a bowl and beat together.

In another, large bowl, mix together the flour, bicarbonate of soda/baking soda, salt and sugar. Pour the wet ingredients into the dry ingredients and swiftly mix together, until just combined. It needs to be quite lumpy but you need to hassle any floury pockets until there are no more.

Drop 1 generous tablespoon of the batter into each paper case. Make a dip in the mixture and spoon in a generous teaspoon of the jam. Divide the remaining batter between the paper cases to cover the jam. Bake in the preheated oven for 18–20 minutes, until well risen. Set aside, still in the tin/pan, to cool for 5 minutes before you apply the topping.

When the muffins have cooled for 5 minutes, brush their tops with the melted butter for the topping and roll in the sugar. Transfer to a wire rack to cool to room temperature.

Cranberry, orange and pistachio muffins

These muffins look so appealing when you pull them out of the oven on a cold winter's morning. The tart tang of the cranberries ensures that the muffins are not too sweet.

2 eggs

80 g/5 tablespoons golden caster/granulated sugar

50 ml/3 tablespoons vegetable or groundnut/peanut oil

finely grated zest and freshly squeezed juice of 1 orange

150 g/1 cup plus 2 tablespoons plain/all-purpose flour

2½ teaspoons baking powder

100 g/¾ cup fresh or frozen cranberries

Topping

50 g/⅓ cup fresh or frozen cranberries

a handful of shelled pistachio nuts, chopped

light brown soft sugar, to sprinkle

a 6-hole muffin tin/pan, lined with paper cases

Makes 6 muffins

Preheat the oven to 180°C (350°F) Gas 4.

Put the eggs, sugar, oil and orange zest and juice in a mixing bowl and mix well until you have a smooth liquid. Mix the flour and baking powder together in a separate bowl, then mix into the wet ingredients. Stir in the cranberries until evenly mixed.

Fill each muffin case about two-thirds full with batter. Scatter the cranberries and pistachio nuts for the topping over the muffins and finish with a sprinkling of sugar. Bake in the preheated oven for about 25 minutes. Do not be tempted to open the oven door halfway through baking as it might cause the muffins to sink. When they are ready, they should be well risen and springy to the touch.

Muffins are always best eaten warm from the oven, but if you have some left over you can refresh them with a quick flash in the microwave. Store in airtight container for 2–3 days.

Wholemeal spelt, carrot, apple and pumpkin seed muffins

2 eggs

80 g/5 tablespoons golden caster/granulated sugar

50 ml/3 tablespoons vegetable or groundnut/peanut oil

150 g/1 cup plus 2 tablespoons wholemeal spelt flour

1½ teaspoons baking powder

1 teaspoon ground cinnamon

1 small carrot, grated

1 small apple, peeled, cored and diced

20 g/2 tablespoons pumpkin seeds

Topping

30 g/3 tablespoons pumpkin seeds

light brown soft sugar, to sprinkle

a 6-hole muffin tin/pan, lined with paper cases

Makes 6 muffins

These wholemeal spelt muffins are delicious – light, nutty and wholesome with hints of cinnamon and apple.

Preheat the oven to 180°C (350°F) Gas 4.

Put the eggs, sugar and oil in a mixing bowl and mix well until you have a smooth liquid. Mix the flour, baking powder and cinnamon together in a separate bowl, then mix into the wet ingredients. Stir in the carrot, apple and pumpkin seeds until evenly mixed.

Fill each muffin case about two-thirds full with batter. Scatter the pumpkin seeds for the topping over the muffins and finish with a sprinkling of sugar. Bake in the preheated oven for about 25 minutes. Do not be tempted to open the oven door halfway through baking as it might cause the muffins to sink. When they are ready, they should be well risen and springy to the touch.

Muffins are always best eaten warm from the oven, but if you have some left over you can refresh them with a quick flash in the microwave. Store in airtight container for 2–3 days.

Passion fruit butterfly cakes

3 passion fruit

115 g/1 stick unsalted butter, at room temperature

115 g/½ cup caster/granulated sugar

2 eggs

115 g/1 cup self-raising flour

1 teaspoon baking powder

To decorate

6 passion fruit

150 g/⅔ cup mascarpone

4 tablespoons icing/confectioners' sugar, sifted, plus extra to dust

a 12-hole cupcake tin/pan, lined with paper cases

Makes 12 cakes

A plateful of these pretty, passion fruit-scented cakes look like a swarm of fluttering butterflies. They hark back to old-fashioned children's tea parties, when it was guaranteed to find a batch of butterfly cakes clustered on the table. They add a touch of vintage style to any party, child or adult.

Preheat the oven to 180°C (350°F) Gas 4.

Halve the passion fruit and scoop the flesh into a sieve/strainer set over a bowl. Press with the back of a teaspoon to extract the juice.

Beat the butter and sugar together in a bowl until pale and fluffy, then beat in the eggs, one at a time. Sift the flour and baking powder into the mixture and fold in. Stir in the passion fruit juice.

Spoon the mixture into the paper cases, then bake in the preheated oven for about 17 minutes until risen and golden and a skewer inserted in the centre comes out clean. Transfer to a wire rack to cool.

To decorate, halve the passion fruit and scoop the flesh into a sieve/strainer set over a bowl. Press with the back of a teaspoon to extract the juice, then add the mascarpone and sugar to the bowl. Mix until smooth and creamy. Cover and refrigerate for about 30 minutes to thicken up.

Slice the top off each cake, then cut each top in half. Spoon a generous dollop of the mascarpone mixture onto each cake, then top with the two halves, setting them at an angle to resemble wings. Dust with icing/confectioners' sugar and serve.

Lavender cupcakes

Subtly scented with lavender, these golden, buttery cupcakes are deliciously simple with an understated elegance, so they're perfect for serving mid-afternoon with a cup of tea. The fragrant taste of the lavender flowers gives the cakes an elusive hint that you can't quite put your finger on.

115 g/½ cup caster/ granulated sugar

¼ teaspoon dried lavender flowers

115 g/1 stick unsalted butter, at room temperature

2 eggs

115 g/1 cup self-raising flour

2 tablespoons milk

To decorate

185 g/1½ cups icing/ confectioners' sugar, sifted

1 egg white

lilac food colouring

12 sprigs of fresh lavender

a 12-hole cupcake tin/pan, lined with paper cases

Makes 12 cakes

Preheat the oven to 180°C (350°F) Gas 4.

Put the sugar and lavender flowers in a food processor and process briefly to combine. Tip the lavender sugar into a bowl with the butter and beat together until pale and fluffy.

Beat the eggs into the butter mixture, one at a time, then sift in the flour and fold in. Stir in the milk.

Spoon the mixture into the paper cases. Bake in the preheated oven for about 18 minutes until risen and golden and a skewer inserted in the centre comes out clean. Transfer to a wire rack to cool.

To decorate, gradually beat the sugar into the egg white in a bowl, then add a few drops of food colouring and stir to achieve a lavender-coloured frosting. Spoon the frosting over the cakes, then top each one with a sprig of fresh lavender. Leave to set before serving.

100 g/½ cup packed light brown soft sugar

160 ml/⅔ cup sunflower oil

2 eggs

grated zest of 1 orange

seeds from 5 cardamom pods, crushed

½ teaspoon ground ginger

200 g/1½ cups self-raising flour

2 carrots, grated

60 g/½ cup shelled walnuts or pecan nuts, roughly chopped

To decorate

150 g/⅔ cup mascarpone

finely grated zest of 1 orange

1½ teaspoons freshly squeezed lemon juice

50 g/⅓ cup icing/confectioners' sugar, sifted

a 12-hole cupcake tin/pan, lined with paper cases

Makes 12 cakes

Carrot and cardamom cupcakes

Lightly spiced and topped with a creamy citrus mascarpone frosting, these delightful little cakes are just the thing when you need a treat. They're not too sweet, but offer just the right combination of crunch, crumble, spice, sweetness and creaminess – plus that little hint of naughtiness that a cupcake should always have.

Preheat the oven to 180°C (350°F) Gas 4.

Put the sugar in a bowl and break up using the back of a fork, then beat in the oil and eggs. Stir in the orange zest, crushed cardamom seeds and ginger, then sift the flour into the mixture and fold in. Add the carrot and nuts and stir through.

Spoon the mixture into the paper cases and bake in the preheated oven for about 20 minutes until risen and a skewer inserted in the centre comes out clean. Transfer to a wire rack to cool.

To decorate, beat the mascarpone, orange zest, lemon juice and sugar together in a bowl and spread over the cakes.

Maple and pecan cupcakes

115 g/1 stick unsalted butter, at room temperature

50 g/¼ cup packed light brown soft sugar

160 ml/⅔ cup maple syrup

2 eggs

115 g/1 cup self-raising flour

60 g/½ cup shelled pecan nuts, roughly chopped

To decorate

60 g/½ cup caster/granulated sugar

12 pecan nut halves

50 g/3 tablespoons unsalted butter, at room temperature

3 tablespoons maple syrup

145 g/1¼ cups icing/confectioners' sugar, sifted

a 12-hole cupcake tin/pan, lined with paper cases

Makes 12 cakes

Maple syrup and pecans are a classic combination, and no better anywhere than in these light, sticky cakes topped with creamy, buttery frosting and caramelized pecans. Look out for the darker, amber maple syrup as it has a more intense flavour that really shines through in the fluffy, buttery sponge.

Preheat the oven to 180°C (350°F) Gas 4.

Beat the butter and sugar together in a bowl until creamy, then beat in the maple syrup. Beat in the eggs, one at a time, then sift the flour into the mixture and fold in, along with the nuts.

Spoon the mixture into the paper cases and bake in the preheated oven for about 17 minutes until risen and golden and a skewer inserted in the centre comes out clean. Transfer to a wire rack to cool.

To make the caramelized pecans, put the caster/granulated sugar in a saucepan and add 2 tablespoons water. Heat gently, stirring, until the sugar melts and dissolves. Increase the heat and boil for about 6 minutes until it turns a pale gold colour. Spread the nuts out on a sheet of baking parchment and spoon over a little of the caramel to cover each nut individually. Leave to cool.

Beat the butter, maple syrup and icing/confectioners' sugar together in a bowl until pale and fluffy. Spread the mixture over the cakes and top each one with a caramelized pecan.

Little almond, polenta and lemon syrup cakes

140 g/1 cup fine polenta/
cornmeal

1 tablespoon baking powder

250 g/1¾ cups ground almonds

225 g/2 sticks unsalted butter,
at room temperature

275 g/1 cup golden caster/
granulated sugar

1 tablespoon very finely grated
lemon zest

4 eggs

Lemon syrup

115 g/½ cup golden
caster/granulated sugar

2 tablespoons freshly squeezed
lemon juice

30 g/3 tablespoons flaked/
slivered almonds, lightly toasted

icing/confectioners' sugar,
to serve

*a 12-hole muffin tin/pan,
lined with paper cases*

Makes 12 cakes

*Polenta is Italian cornmeal and it comes in various grades,
ranging from coarse to fine – use a very fine grade here
(which can be found at any Italian deli) for a good dense
texture. It's best to eat these cakes on the day you make them,
but that shouldn't be too difficult!*

Preheat the oven to 180°C (350°F) Gas 4.

Sift the polenta, baking powder and ground almonds into a large
mixing bowl. Tip any pieces of husk into the bowl and make a well
in the centre.

In a separate bowl, beat the butter, sugar and lemon zest together until
pale and creamy. Add the eggs one at a time, beating well after each
addition. Gradually fold in the polenta mixture until well combined.

Spoon the mixture into the prepared muffin tin/pan, dividing evenly.
Bake in the preheated oven for 25 minutes, until risen and golden.
Remove from the oven and let cool in the tin/pan for 10 minutes.
Carefully transfer the cakes to a wire rack set over a baking sheet
(to catch any drips of syrup later on).

To make the syrup, put the sugar, lemon juice and 2 tablespoons cold
water in a small saucepan. Set over low heat and cook, stirring, until
the sugar dissolves. Increase the heat to high and bring to the boil, then
reduce the heat to a low simmer and cook for 2–3 minutes, until syrupy.

Pour the syrup over the warm cakes and sprinkle the flaked/slivered
almonds on top so they stick to the syrup. Let cool and dust with
icing/confectioners' sugar just before serving.

Pear and chocolate muffins

100 g/3½ oz. dark/bittersweet chocolate, broken into pieces

100 g/7 tablespoons unsalted butter

200 g/1 cup caster/granulated sugar

200 g/7 oz. cream cheese (not low-fat)

2 eggs

200 g/1½ cups plain/all-purpose flour

1½ teaspoons baking powder

1 teaspoon ground cinnamon

a pinch of fine sea salt

400 g/14 oz. ripe pears (about 2–3), such as Williams, peeled, cored and diced

100 g dark/bittersweet chocolate chips

a 12-hole muffin tin/pan, lined with paper cases

Makes 12 muffins

Pears have the fortunate ability to partner chocolate possibly better than any other fruit. In this recipe they snuggle up to lots of rich chocolate and tangy cream cheese, and some cinnamon adds a pleasing spiciness to the mix.

Preheat the oven to 190°C (375°F) Gas 5.

Put the chocolate and butter in a heatproof bowl and set it over a large saucepan of simmering water – do not let the bottom of the bowl touch the water. Stir gently as it melts. Remove the bowl from the heat just before it has melted completely and allow it to finish melting in the residual heat. Set aside until needed.

Combine the sugar and cream cheese in a mixing bowl. Beat with a hand-held electric whisk until well blended. Add the eggs and melted chocolate mixture and continue beating until well blended.

Combine all the dry ingredients in a separate bowl and mix well. Tip into the chocolate mixture and, with the whisk on low, mix until just blended. Fold in the pears and chocolate chips. Spoon the mixture into the paper cases, dividing it evenly.

Bake in the preheated oven until a skewer inserted in the centre of a muffin comes out almost clean, about 20–30 minutes. Transfer to a wire rack and let cool before serving.

Cranberry and white chocolate cupcakes

60 g/½ stick butter, at room temperature

60 g/⅓ cup caster/granulated sugar

1 egg

60 g/½ cup self-raising flour plus 1 teaspoon baking powder

30 g/⅓ cup pecans, finely ground

60 g/½ cup dried cranberries

50 g/⅓ cup white chocolate chips

2 tablespoons buttermilk

Frosting

220 g/1½ cups icing/confectioners' sugar

115 g/1 stick butter, at room temperature

1 teaspoon vanilla extract

1 tablespoon buttermilk

pink food colouring

sprinkles of your choice

a 12-hole cupcake tin/pan, lined with paper cases

a piping bag, fitted with a large star nozzle/tip

Makes 12 cakes

Everyone loves a cupcake. These are bursting with cranberries and white chocolate and topped with a pretty swirled buttermilk frosting – perfect for any celebration.

Preheat the oven to 180°C (350°F) Gas 4.

Put the butter and sugar in a mixing bowl and whisk until light and creamy. Add the egg and whisk again. Fold in the flour, baking powder, ground pecans, cranberries, chocolate chips and buttermilk using a spatula or large spoon. Divide the batter between the paper cases. Bake in the preheated oven for 15–20 minutes, until the cakes are golden brown and spring back to the touch. Transfer to a wire rack to cool.

To make the frosting, sift the icing/confectioners' sugar into a mixing bowl and add the butter, vanilla extract and buttermilk. Beat together until you have a thick frosting. Put half the frosting in a separate bowl and mix in a few drops of pink food colouring. Spoon the frosting into the piping bag, spreading the pink one along one side of the bag and the cream one along the other side so that when you squeeze it the frosting is striped. Pipe a generous swirl of frosting onto each cake, add some sprinkles and dust with icing/confectioners' sugar.

These cupcakes are best eaten on the day they are made.

Exploding berry crumble muffins

375 g/2¾ cups plain/
all-purpose flour

3 teaspoons baking powder

1 teaspoon bicarbonate
of soda/baking soda

150 g/¾ cup golden caster/
granulated sugar

½ teaspoon salt

2 eggs, beaten

115 g/1 stick unsalted
butter, melted

200 g/¾ cup sour cream

60 ml/¼ cup whole milk

180 g/1¼ cups raspberries

Topping

100 g/¾ cup plain/
all-purpose flour

75 g/5 tablespoons butter,
chilled and cubed

30 g/2 tablespoons golden
caster/granulated sugar

30 g/3 tablespoons
flaked/slivered almonds

*a 12-hole muffin tin/pan, top
greased and lined with paper
muffin cases*

Makes 12 muffins

*These look like the voluptuous muffins which are sold in cafés
and which seem to have exploded out of their tins with their
generous proportions. There is no secret trick to this – just fill
the muffin cases up to the top. Make sure you grease the top of
the muffin tin/pan so that any overflowing muffin will not stick.*

Preheat the oven to 170°C (375°F) Gas 3.

To make the topping, put the flour and butter in a food processor and
pulse briefly, just until the butter is blended. Tip out into a bowl and add
the sugar and almonds, pressing the mixture together with your hands.

To make the muffins, sift the flour, baking powder, bicarbonate of soda/
baking soda, sugar and salt into a large mixing bowl. Put the eggs in a
small jug/pitcher, add the melted butter, sour cream and milk and
whisk to combine. Pour the wet ingredients into the
dry ingredients and scatter the raspberries on top.
Using a large spoon, fold until the mixture is
moistened. It needs to be lumpy and shouldn't
be overworked otherwise the baked muffins
will be tough. Spoon into the paper cases right
to the top. For regular-sized (not exploding!)
muffins you can spoon the cases two-thirds full –
you will be able to make more of these with this
amount of mixture. Finish by scattering over the
topping. Bake in the preheated oven for 25–28
minutes for large muffins, or 18–22 minutes for
the smaller ones.

Leave to cool for 5 minutes in the tin/pan before
transferring to a wire rack.

140 g/1 cup plain/
all-purpose flour

85 g/⅓ cup plain wholemeal/
wholewheat flour

145 g/1 cup dark brown sugar

1 teaspoon bicarbonate
of soda/baking soda

¼ teaspoon baking powder

1 teaspoon ground cinnamon

½ teaspoon each ground
nutmeg, ginger and cloves

a pinch of fine sea salt

250 ml/1 cup buttermilk

125 ml/½ cup vegetable oil

1 teaspoon vanilla extract

1 tart apple, such as Cox's or
Granny Smith, peeled, cored
and finely chopped

50 g/2 oz. raisins

Frosting

400 g/16 oz. cream cheese
(not low-fat)

115 g/1 stick unsalted butter,
at room temperature

120 g/1 cup icing/
confectioners' sugar

1 teaspoon vanilla extract

*a 12-hole muffin tin/pan,
lined with paper cases*

Makes 12 muffins

Apple spice muffins

*A virtuous but tasty mix of apples, raisins,
buttermilk and warm spices, these muffins are
great for breakfast, brunch or lunch boxes.
They are the perfect fragrant treat for eerie
Halloween nights and cold, wintery days. .*

For the frosting, put the cream cheese, butter, sugar and
vanilla in a bowl and beat with a hand-held electric whisk
until smooth. Refrigerate until needed.

Preheat the oven to 180°C (350°F) Gas 4. In a large mixing
bowl, combine the plain/all-purpose flour, wholemeal/
wholewheat flour, sugar, bicarbonate of soda/baking soda,
baking powder, cinnamon, nutmeg, ginger, cloves and salt
and mix well to combine.

In a separate bowl, combine the buttermilk, oil and vanilla
extract. Stir, then add this mixture to the dry ingredients,
folding in with a spatula to blend thoroughly. Add the apple
and raisins and mix just to combine.

Drop spoonfuls of the mixture into the paper cases, filling
each almost to the top. Bake in the preheated oven until
puffed and a skewer inserted in the centre of a muffin
comes out clean, about 25–35 minutes.

Transfer to a wire rack, let cool completely then spread
the top of each muffin with frosting before serving.

Chocolate and peanut butter are a well-loved combination –you can even buy them in a jar together! These little fairy cakes will please fans of both. But, if you are cooking for friends, remember to label them clearly so anyone with an allergy to peanuts can avoid them.

Little peanut butter cakes

75 g/¼ cup best-quality smooth peanut butter (with no-added sugar)

25 g/2 tablespoons unsalted butter, very soft

100 g/¼ cup firm-packed light muscovado/light brown soft sugar

2 large eggs

½ teaspoon vanilla extract

125 g/1 cup plain/all-purpose flour, sifted

1 teaspoon baking powder

4 tablespoons milk

75 g/½ cup dark/bittersweet chocolate chips, plus extra for decorating

icing/confectioners' sugar, for dusting (optional)

a 12-hole muffin tin/pan, lined with paper cases

a pastry brush (optional)

Makes 12 cakes

Preheat the oven to 180°C (350°F) Gas 4.

Put the peanut butter, butter and sugar in a large mixing bowl and beat with a hand-held electric whisk until smooth.

In a separate bowl combine the eggs and the vanilla extract and whisk together. Add the eggs to the mixing bowl a little at a time, stirring in between until all combined.

Add the flour, baking powder and milk to the bowl and gently stir into the other ingredients. When well mixed, add the chocolate chips and stir thoroughly to mix.

Spoon the mixture into the paper cases until they are about one-third full, sprinkle with chocolate chips and bake in the preheated oven for 15–20 minutes, until a light golden colour. Remove them from the oven and leave to cool on a wire rack.

To decorate, cut a simple shape, such as a heart or star, out of paper to make a stencil. Hold your stencil over each cake and use a pastry brush dipped in a little milk or water to slightly moisten the area where you want the icing/confectioners' sugar to stick. Lift off the stencil. Dust some icing/confectioners' sugar over the cakes then shake each cake to remove the excess sugar and the shape will appear. When cold, store your cakes in an airtight container and eat them within 4 days.

Triple chocolate cupside-down cakes

200 g/1¾ sticks unsalted butter, at room temperature

150 g/¾ cup brown sugar

3 eggs

70 g/2½ oz. milk chocolate, chopped into chunks

70 g/2½ oz. white chocolate, chopped into chunks

1 teaspoon vanilla extract

160 g/1¼ cups self-raising flour

40 g/¼ cup cocoa powder

¼ teaspoon baking powder

White chocolate ganache

100 g/3½ oz. white chocolate, chopped

80 ml/⅓ cup crème fraîche or sour cream

Dark chocolate ganache

60 g/2½ oz. dark/bittersweet chocolate, chopped

120 ml/scant ½ cup double/heavy cream

1 teaspoon icing/confectioners' sugar (optional)

These are really chocolatey mini cakes drizzled with fresh cream chocolate ganache, rather than classic American-style cupcakes piled high with a sweet, whipped frosting. They look most irresistible when half a batch are decorated with a white chocolate ganache and the other half with alluring dark, all with a provocative raspberry dotted on top.

Preheat the oven to 180°C (350°F) Gas 4.

Cream the butter and sugar together in a large bowl with a handheld electric mixer, until creamy and light in colour. Gradually add the eggs to the sugar and butter mixture. Then add the chopped milk and white chocolates and vanilla extract and stir in with a wooden spoon.

Sift in the flour, cocoa powder and baking powder and fold in using a tablespoon. (Do not overwork the cake mixture as it will make your cakes heavy.)

Spoon the mixture into the paper cases, leaving a little space at the top for the cakes to rise.

Bake in the preheated oven for about 20 minutes, until a skewer inserted in the centre of a cake comes out clean and the sponge bounces back when lightly pressed. Leave to cool in the tin/pan for a few minutes before transferring to a wire rack to cool completely.

Make up the ganaches as required. (Simply double the quantities if you are making just one type.) Put the chocolate, crème fraîche and icing/confectioners' sugar (if using, it's optional for a dark ganache) in a small heavy-based saucepan set over low heat. Stir gently until the chocolate melts into the cream. Take off the heat and leave for a few minutes to cool and thicken slightly before using.

To decorate

fresh raspberries

natural glacé cherries

white and milk chocolate curls

dragées or sprinkles

*a 12-hole cupcake tin/pan,
lined with paper cases*

Makes 12 cakes

Peel the paper cases off the cakes and turn them upside down on the wire rack. (Slide a piece of baking parchment underneath to catch any drips.) Pour a little of the ganache onto what is now the top of each cake and allow it to drizzle down the sides.

Decoration is entirely up to you; choose from fresh raspberries, natural glacé cherries, white and milk chocolate curls, dragées or sprinkles. Put your chosen decoration on the top of the cakes at this stage as the ganache cools and sets. (If your ganache has thickened too much, add a little warm cream to loosen it.)

When cooled, the cupcakes will keep stored in an airtight container in the fridge for up to 2 days.

Large
Cakes

Lime drizzle cake with coconut frosting

175 g/1½ sticks butter, at room temperature

175 g/¾ cup caster/granulated sugar

175 g/1⅓ cups self-raising flour, sifted

3 eggs

finely grated zest of 2 limes

Lime drizzle

75 g/½ cup icing/confectioners' sugar

freshly squeezed juice of 2 limes

Coconut frosting

175 g/6 oz. cream cheese

5 tablespoons coconut cream

2 tablespoons icing/confectioners' sugar

grated zest of 1 lime

an 18-cm/7-inch round cake tin/pan, lightly buttered and base-lined with baking parchment

Serves 8

If you want to make this look extra special, add a few shavings of toasted fresh coconut to the top.

Preheat the oven to 180°C (350°F) Gas 4.

Put the butter, sugar, flour, eggs and lime zest in an electric mixer (or use a large mixing bowl and an electric whisk) and beat until combined.

Spoon the mixture into the prepared tin/pan and spread it evenly with a spatula. Bake in the preheated oven for 50–55 minutes, or until a skewer comes out clean when inserted into the centre of the cake.

Meanwhile, to make the lime drizzle, sift the icing/confectioners' sugar into a bowl and stir in the lime juice, then set aside.

To make the coconut frosting, whisk the cream cheese, coconut cream and icing/confectioners' sugar together in a bowl, then refrigerate until needed.

When the cake is ready, remove it from the oven and, using a small, fine skewer, make a few holes over the surface of the cake. Spoon over the lime drizzle (put the tin/pan on a plate first if it is loose-based). Leave the cake to cool completely in its tin/pan.

Once cold, pop the cake out of the tin/pan, remove the base paper and spread the frosting over the top. Sprinkle with the lime zest.

125 g/¾ cup plain/
all-purpose flour

250 g/1 cup caster/
superfine sugar

10 egg whites

1 teaspoon cream of tartar

½ teaspoon vanilla extract

a punnet/pint of blueberries or 6
ripe peaches, to serve (optional)

Frosting

115 g/½ cup caster/
superfine sugar

2 egg whites

2 teaspoons golden/corn syrup

½ teaspoon vanilla extract

*a 25-cm/10-in ring mould or a
non-stick tube tin/pan, lightly
greased*

Serves 8–12

Angel food cake

*This pure white, whisked sponge cake is the classic all-American
cake. It's traditionally baked in a ring-shaped tin/pan and tastes
divine served with blueberries or juicy wedges of ripe peach.*

Preheat the oven to 180°C (350°F) Gas 4.

In a large bowl, sift together the flour and half the sugar three times,
until very light. Set aside.

In a separate, grease-free bowl, whisk the egg whites with the cream
of tartar until stiff, then gradually whisk in the remaining sugar until
the mixture is thick and glossy. Whisk in the vanilla extract.

Sift half the flour and sugar mixture into the egg whites and gently fold
in, then sift in the remaining flour and fold in.

Spoon the cake mixture into the prepared mould/tube pan and bake
for about 40 minutes, until a skewer inserted into the cake comes out
clean. Turn the cake out on to a wire rack and leave to cool completely
before frosting.

To make the frosting, put the sugar in a saucepan with 4 tablespoons
water and heat, stirring until the sugar dissolves, then boil until the
temperature reaches 240°F (115°C).

In a clean, grease-free bowl, whisk the egg whites until very stiff, then
gradually pour the sugar syrup into the egg whites in a thin stream,
whisking constantly until thick and glossy. Whisk in the golden/corn
syrup and vanilla extract and continue whisking until the frosting has
cooled. Use a palette knife to spread it over the cooled cake. Serve
with blueberries or slices of fresh peach, as preferred.

This recipe also works well using damson jam. Either way, treat yourself to some chilled Greek yogurt on the side.

Blackcurrant, berry and hazelnut crumble cake

150 g/1¼ sticks butter, softened

175 g/¾ cup granulated sugar

2 large eggs

125 g/1 cup self-raising flour

50 g/⅓ cup polenta/cornmeal

1 teaspoon baking powder

finely grated zest of 1 lemon

50 g/¼ cup Greek yogurt

175 g/¾ cup blackcurrant jam

175 g/1¼ cups raspberries

Crumble topping

100 g/⅔ cup shelled, blanched whole hazelnuts

75 g/⅓ cup demerara sugar

75 g/5 tablespoons butter, chilled and cubed

100 g/¾ cup self-raising flour

a 23-cm/9-in springform cake tin/pan, greased and base-lined with baking parchment

Serves 12

Preheat the oven to 180°C (350°F) Gas 4.

To make the crumble topping, chop the nuts by hand or pulse them in a food processor – you want them to be roughly chopped. Mix the sugar, butter and flour in an electric mixer until combined, then add 2 dessertspoons cold water and briefly whizz again until the mixture resembles breadcrumbs. Mix in the nuts. Alternatively, you can rub the butter into the flour by hand in a mixing bowl, then stir in the sugar, water and nuts. Set aside.

Put the butter, sugar, eggs, flour, polenta/cornmeal, baking powder, lemon zest and yogurt in an electric mixer and mix until combined.

Spoon the mixture into the prepared tin/pan and spread it evenly. Tip the jam into a bowl and mix it with a spoon to loosen it, then put spoonfuls over the top of the cake mixture. Using the tip of a round-bladed knife, gently spread the jam by lightly swirling it into the top of the cake mixture. Sprinkle a third of the crumble mixture on top, scatter the raspberries over this, then finish with the remaining crumble topping.

Put the tin/pan on a baking sheet and bake in the preheated oven for 1 hour 5 minutes–1 hour 10 minutes, until just set in the middle. Leave to cool in the tin/pan before releasing it, removing the base paper and transferring to a plate or board to slice.

75 g/½ cup glacé cherries, chopped, plus extra, whole, to decorate

50 g/¼ cup candied mixed peel

450 g/1 lb. mixed dried fruit (such as currants, raisins, chopped dried apricots)

225 g/1¾ cups plain/all-purpose flour

1 teaspoon baking powder

1 teaspoon mixed/apple pie spice

a pinch of salt

175 g/1½ sticks unsalted butter, at room temperature

175 g/¾ cup caster/granulated sugar

3 eggs, lightly beaten

25 g/¼ cup ground almonds

2–3 tablespoons milk

apricot jam, chopped dried apricots, blanched almonds, pecan halves, to decorate

a deep, 20-cm/8-inch round cake tin/pan

Serves 8–10

Easy fruit cake

This is a simple fruit cake that can be decorated any number of ways, but with its crown of sparkling, jewelled dried fruits, it makes a majestic teatime treat.

Preheat the oven to 170°C (325°F) Gas 3. Line the base and side of the cake tin/pan with a double thickness of baking parchment.

Mix the chopped glacé cherries, mixed peel and dried fruit together in a bowl. Sift the flour, baking powder, mixed spice and salt together in another bowl.

Put the butter and sugar in the bowl of an electric mixer (or use a large bowl and an electric whisk). Cream them until pale and light. Gradually add the beaten eggs, mixing well between each addition and scraping down the sides of the bowl with a rubber spatula from time to time. Add the dried fruit and stir to mix. Add the sifted dry ingredients and the ground almonds to the mixture and fold in using a large metal spoon or rubber spatula. Add the milk and mix until smooth.

Spoon the mixture into the prepared cake tin/pan and spread evenly. Put the tin/pan on the middle shelf of the preheated oven. Bake for 30 minutes, then turn the heat down to 150°C (300°F) Gas 2. Continue to bake for a further 1½ hours, or until a skewer inserted into the middle of the cake comes out clean. Remove the cake from the oven and leave to cool in the tin/pan. Once the cake is completely cold, tip it out of the tin/pan and carefully peel off the paper.

Put about 5 tablespoons of apricot jam in a small saucepan over low heat. Leave until runny, then sieve/strain.

Brush the top of the cake with a thin layer of the jam. Arrange the glacé cherries, apricots and nuts in a pretty pattern on top. Brush with a little more jam to glaze, then leave to set.

Victoria sandwich cake

180 g/1½ sticks butter, at room temperature

180 g/¾ cup plus 2 tablespoons caster/superfine sugar

3 eggs

180 g/1⅓ cups self-raising flour

3½ tablespoons good-quality raspberry jam

140 g/1 cup fresh raspberries

120 ml/½ cup whipping cream

icing/confectioners' sugar, for dusting

2 x 20-cm/8-inch round cake tins/pans, greased and base-lined with baking parchment

Serves 8

It's hard to beat a freshly baked, golden, buttery Victoria sponge filled with fresh raspberries and cream. Other juicy berries such as strawberries or blueberries are equally delicious, together with the equivalent jam.

Preheat the oven to 180°C (350°F) Gas 4.

Put the butter and sugar in a mixing bowl and beat together until pale and fluffy. Beat in the eggs one at a time. Sift in the flour and mix to combine.

Spoon the cake mixture into the prepared tins/pans and level the surface using the back of the spoon. Bake in the preheated oven for 20–25 minutes until golden brown and the centre of the sponge springs back when lightly pressed. Turn the cakes out on to a wire rack, gently peel off the lining paper and leave to cool completely.

To serve, use a spatula to spread the jam over one cake and top with the raspberries. Whip the cream until it stands in soft peaks, then spread it over the raspberries. Put the second cake on top and dust with icing/confectioners' sugar.

225 g/1½ cups self-raising flour

1 teaspoon baking powder

1 teaspoon ground cinnnamon

½ teaspoon ground ginger

¼ teaspoon freshly grated nutmeg

150 ml/⅔ cups sunflower oil

3 eggs

200 g/1 cup light brown soft sugar

350 g/2 cups grated carrot

grated zest of 1 orange

60 g/⅓ cup roasted, unsalted pistachio nuts, roughly chopped

Topping

200 g/7 oz. cream cheese

75 g/½ cup icing/confectioners' sugar

1½ teaspoons lemon juice

grated zest of 1 lemon

chopped unsalted pistachio nuts

crystallized violet and/or rose petals

a 20-cm/8-in cake tin/pan, greased and lined with baking parchment

Serves 8

Spiced carrot and pistachio cake

There's something comforting and homely about carrot cake, but with the added dash of vibrant green pistachio nuts and romantic flower petals this humble cake is transformed into an indulgent centrepiece. The lemony cream cheese frosting is just the icing on the cake.

Preheat the oven to 180°C (350°F) Gas 4.

Sift the flour, baking powder and spices into a large bowl and make a well in the centre. In a separate bowl, beat together the oil, eggs and sugar. Pour this mixture into the dry ingredients and fold together. Add the grated carrot, orange zest and nuts and mix. Spoon the mixture into the prepared cake tin/pan, level out the surface and bake in the preheated oven for about 1 hour, or until a skewer inserted in the centre comes out clean. Leave to cool in the tin/pan for 10 minutes, then turn out on to a wire rack to cool.

To make the lemon frosting, beat together the cream cheese, icing/confectioners' sugar and the lemon juice and zest until smooth and creamy. Spread over the cooled cake, then decorate with pistachios and crystallized petals.

225 g/2 sticks unsalted butter, at room temperature

300 g/1½ cups granulated sugar

4 eggs, beaten

2 teaspoons vanilla extract

finely grated zest of 1 lemon

375 g/2 cups plain/all-purpose flour

2 teaspoons baking powder

1 teaspoon bicarbonate of soda/baking soda

a pinch of salt

200 ml/¾ cup buttermilk

6 tablespoons strawberry jam

2 quantities Frosting (page 66), but using seeds scraped out of a vanilla pod in place of the cinnamon

200 g/ 6 oz. white chocolate, coarsely grated

350 g/2½ cups small strawberries and/or fraises des bois/wild strawberries (if possible)

250 g/1½ cups raspberries

125 g/1 cup redcurrants, crystallized

2 x 20-cm/8-inch round cake tins/pans, greased and base-lined with baking parchment

Serves 8

High summer cake

This is essentially a grown-up Victoria Sponge with a few added extras. A glorious addition to any summer table.

Preheat the oven to 180°C (350°F) Gas 4.

In a mixing bowl, beat together the butter and sugar until light and creamy. Gradually add the beaten eggs, mixing well between each addition. Add the vanilla and lemon zest and mix again.

Sift together the flour, baking powder, bicarbonate of soda/baking soda and salt. Add to the cake mixture with the buttermilk and mix again until smooth.

Divide the mixture between the prepared cake tins/pans and bake on the middle shelf of the preheated oven for about 35 minutes, or until well risen, golden and a skewer inserted into the middle of the cakes comes out clean. Leave to cool in the tins/pans for 5 minutes, then transfer to a wire rack to cool completely.

Cut the cold cakes in half horizontally, using a long, serrated knife. Place one layer on a serving plate and spread with 2 tablespoons of the strawberry jam. Spread 2 tablespoons of the frosting over the jam and top with another cake layer. Repeat with the remaining cake layers, leaving the top layer plain. Gently press the cake layers together. Cover the side of the cake with frosting, spreading evenly with a palette knife.

Scatter the grated white chocolate onto a tray and, holding the cake very carefully, roll the side in the grated chocolate to coat completely. Spread a thick layer of frosting on top of the cake and finish with the mixed berries and crystallized redcurrants. Serve immediately.

Devilishly delicious chocolate cake

225 ml/scant 1 cup whole milk

1 tablespoon freshly squeezed lemon juice

200 g/1½ cups plain/all-purpose flour

1 teaspoon bicarbonate of soda/baking powder

75 g/½ cup cocoa powder

100 g/6½ tablespoons unsalted butter, at room temperature

225 g/1 cup plus 2 tablespoons golden caster/granulated sugar

3 eggs, lightly beaten

chocolate curls, to decorate

Frosting

200 g/7 oz. dark/bittersweet chocolate, chopped

250 g/1 cup mascarpone

1–2 tablespoons icing/confectioners' sugar, sifted

2 x 20-cm/8-inch round cake tins/pans, greased

Serves 8

This cake is so mouth-wateringly good that it would be a sin not to try it. Yes, it's rich, but oh so lovely for any celebration!

Preheat the oven to 180°C (350°F) Gas 4.

Pour the milk into a jug/pitcher, add the lemon juice and leave to sour while you prepare the rest of the ingredients.

Sift the flour, bicarbonate of soda and cocoa powder together into a bowl. Cream the butter and sugar together in a separate large bowl until creamy and light in colour. Gradually add the eggs to the sugar and butter mixture. Alternately fold the soured milk and flour into the egg mixture, until everything is mixed together.

Divide the mixture between the prepared baking tins/pans and tap them to ensure they are level. Bake in the preheated oven for about 25 minutes, until a skewer inserted in the centre comes out clean. Leave the cakes to cool in the tins/pans for about 10 minutes before turning out onto a wire rack to cool.

For the frosting, melt the chocolate in a heatproof bowl set over a saucepan of gently simmering water. Take the bowl off the pan and leave to cool for 5 minutes. Add the mascarpone and icing/confectioners' sugar to taste (add 1 tablespoon for a relatively sharp frosting but 2 for a sweeter one). Beat until light and fluffy, ideally using a handheld electric mixer.

Working quickly, as the frosting will quickly start to set, sandwich the cakes together with half of the frosting and cover the cake with the remainder. Decorate as you wish with white and milk chocolate curls, sprinkles, traditional sweets, candles or even sparklers.

Coffee and walnut cake

180 g/1½ sticks butter, at room temperature

180 g/¾ cup caster/granulated sugar

3 eggs

180 g/1 cup self-raising flour

2 teaspoons instant coffee granules, dissolved in 1 tablespoon hot water

60 g/½ cup walnut pieces

Frosting

250 g/9 oz. mascarpone

85 g/½ cup icing/confectioners' sugar, sifted

1½ teaspoons instant coffee granules, dissolved in 1½ teaspoons hot water

walnut halves, to decorate

2 x 20-cm/8-inch round cake tins/pans, greased and base-lined with baking parchment

Serves 8–12

This classic teatime cake is enduringly popular, perhaps because something magical happens when coffee and walnuts come together.

Preheat the oven to 180°C (350°F) Gas 4.

Put the butter and sugar in a large bowl and cream together until pale and fluffy. Beat in the eggs one at a time. Sift the flour into the butter mixture and stir to combine. Fold in the walnuts and coffee. Divide the cake mixture between the two prepared tins/pans and level out the surface of each.

Bake in the preheated oven for 20–25 minutes until golden and the sponge springs back when gently pressed or a skewer inserted in the centre comes out clean. Transfer to a wire rack, carefully peel off the paper and let cool completely before frosting.

To make the frosting, beat together the mascarpone, icing/confectioners' sugar and coffee until smooth and creamy. Spread slightly less than half of the frosting over one of the cooled cakes, then place the second cake on top. Spread the remaining frosting over the top and decorate with walnut halves to finish.

Queen of Sheba chocolate and almond cake

100 g/3½ oz. dark/bittersweet chocolate, chopped

100 g/6½ tablespoons unsalted butter, at room temperature

100 g/½ cup plus 1 tablespoon golden caster/granulated sugar,

2 tablespoons rum or coffee

¼ teaspoon bitter almond extract

3 eggs, separated

50 g/½ cup ground almonds

a pinch of salt

50 g/⅓ cup plain/all-purpose flour

2 tablespoons unsweetened cocoa powder, plus extra to dust

golden chocolate dragées, to decorate

fresh geranium petals, to decorate

a 20-cm/8-in springform cake tin/pan, greased, based-lined with baking parchment and dusted with flour

Serves 6–8

This romantically named classic French cake is all that you expect the enigmatic Queen of Sheba, who stole the heart of King Solomon, to have been – rich, dark and tempting. Veiled in darkest cocoa, adorned with gold dragées and strewn with deep geranium petals, the cake reveals a soft, moist centre.

Preheat the oven to 180°C (350°F) Gas 4.

Melt the chocolate in a small bowl over a saucepan filled with hot water, or in a microwave.

Using an electric whisk/mixer, cream the butter and sugar in a large bowl until really pale and fluffy, then beat in the rum and almond extract followed by the egg yolks, one by one. Working quickly, fold the chocolate into the mixture, then stir in the ground almonds.

Using a clean electric whisk/mixer, beat the egg whites with the salt in a clean, dry bowl until they form floppy peaks, then sprinkle in the remaining tablespoon of sugar and beat again until the mixture forms stiff peaks. Beat a spoonful into the chocolate mixture with a metal spoon to loosen it, then fold in half of the egg whites. Sift the flour and cocoa onto the mixture, then gently fold in. Finally, fold in the remaining egg whites.

Pour the mixture into the cake tin/pan, spreading it out evenly over the base. Bake for 20–25 minutes. Check it after 20 minutes – the cake should be risen and a bit wobbly in the centre, but firm around the edges. Remove from the oven and leave to cool in the tin/pan for 10 minutes. Loosen the sides with a knife and turn out onto a wire rack to cool completely. When cold, dust the top evenly with cocoa and decorate with the gold dragées and geranium petals.

Courgette, lemon and poppyseed cake with lemon butter frosting

30 g/3 tablespoons poppyseeds

finely grated zest of 2 lemons

80 ml/⅓ cup milk

250 g/2 sticks unsalted butter, at room temperature

280 g/1½ cup light brown soft sugar

4 large eggs, separated

½ teaspoon vanilla extract

200 g/1½ cups self-raising flour, sifted

80 g/⅔ cup almonds, blanched and ground

250 g/8 oz. courgette/zucchini, topped, tailed and coarsely grated

½ teaspoon cream of tartar

Frosting

220 g/1 cup icing/confectioners' sugar

25 g/2 tablespoons butter, melted

2–3 tablespoons freshly squeezed lemon juice

1 teaspoon finely grated lemon zest

a 23-cm/9-in springform cake tin/pan, greased and lined with baking parchment

Serves 8–10

There is a lovely retro charm, redolent of 1950s cookbooks, about making a sweet cake with a vegetable that's usually served savoury. The courgette/zucchini performs the same function as grated carrot does in the more familiar carrot cake. It keeps this cake wonderfully fresh and moist.

Preheat the oven to 190°C (375°F) Gas 5.

Put the poppyseeds and lemon zest in a small bowl. Heat the milk until hot (easiest in the microwave), stir it into the poppyseed mixture and let it cool while you make the cake mixture.

Cream the butter and sugar together until very light and fluffy. Beat in the egg yolks, one at a time, followed by the vanilla extract, flour and almonds. Fold in the courgette/zucchini followed by the poppyseed mixture. In a separate, grease-free bowl, whisk the eggs whites with the cream of tartar until stiff, then fold the egg whites into the cake mixture. Scrape the mixture into the prepared tin/pan, smooth down and bake in the centre of the preheated oven for 50–60 minutes until the cake is just firm to the touch and a skewer inserted into the centre comes out clean with no uncooked mixture sticking to it. Let the cake cool in the tin/pan for 10 minutes before turning onto a wire rack.

When cool, sift the icing/confectioners' sugar into a bowl, make a well in the centre and add the still-hot melted butter. Start to mix, adding sufficient lemon juice to make a spreadable icing. Mix in the lemon zest, then spread over the cake. Leave for 1–2 hours to set before serving.

Cinnamon blueberry cake

175 g/1½ sticks unsalted butter

175 g/¾ cup granulated sugar

4 large eggs, lightly beaten

a pinch of ground cinnamon

175 g/1⅓ cups self-raising flour, sifted

2 teaspoons baking powder

a pinch of salt

225 g/1 pint blueberries

Cinnamon frosting

200 g/6½ oz. cream cheese, chilled

100 g/a scant ½ cup crème fraîche or double/heavy cream, chilled

50 g/3 tablespoons unsalted butter, softened and cubed

150 g/1 cup icing/confectioners' sugar, plus extra for dusting

2 teaspoons ground cinnamon

2 x 20-cm/8-inch round cake tins/pans, greased and base-lined with baking parchment

Serves 8

Make this cake on the day you are going to eat it, but let it cool completely before assembling and serving.

Preheat the oven to 180°C (350°F) Gas 4.

Put the butter and sugar in an electric mixer (or use a large mixing bowl and an electric whisk) and beat for 3–4 minutes, or until pale and fluffy. Gradually add the beaten eggs with the beaters still running, followed by the cinnamon, flour, baking powder and salt. Mix until all the ingredients are combined.

Divide the mixture between the prepared tins/pans and spread it evenly with a spatula. Bake in the preheated oven for 20–25 minutes, or until lightly golden and risen. Leave to cool in the tins/pans for 30 minutes. Tip the cakes out onto a wire rack and peel off the base papers. Leave to cool completely.

To make the cinnamon frosting, whisk all the ingredients together to combine.

To assemble, place one cake on a cake stand or large serving plate and spread two-thirds of the cinnamon frosting over the top – a spatula or table knife is the ideal tool to use here. Scatter three-quarters of the blueberries on top of the frosting.

Place the other cake on the blueberries and spread the remaining frosting over the top. Finish with the rest of the blueberries and dust with a little icing/confectioners' sugar.

Spiced oatmeal cake with chocolate and cinnamon frosting

80 g/⅔ cup rolled oats

125 g/1 stick unsalted butter, at room temperature

230 g/2¼ cups light brown soft sugar

230 g/1 cup caster/granulated sugar

2 eggs

185 g/1⅓ cups plain/all-purpose flour

1 teaspoon baking powder

1 teaspoon ground cinnamon

¼ teaspoon freshly grated nutmeg

Frosting

200 ml/¾ cup light/single cream

200 g/6 oz. dark/bittersweet chocolate, broken into small pieces

½ teaspoon ground cinnamon

a 20-cm/8-inch springform cake tin/pan, greased and base-lined with baking parchment

Serves 10–12

This is a dense and richly spiced cake and not one for the fainthearted. The finger-licking ganache is good enough to eat on its own, but do try and save some for the cake!

Preheat the oven to 180°C (350°F) Gas 4.

Put the oats in a heatproof bowl. Add 300 ml/1¼ cups boiling water and stir. Cover with clingfilm/plastic wrap and let sit for 20 minutes.

Put the butter and both sugars in a mixing bowl and beat together until pale, thick and creamy. Add one of the eggs and beat until well combined. Add the remaining egg and beat again. Stir in the flour, baking powder, cinnamon and nutmeg, then fold in the softened oats. Spoon the mixture into the prepared cake tin/pan and level the surface.

Bake in the preheated oven for 35–40 minutes, until golden. Let cool in the tin/pan for 10 minutes, then transfer to a wire rack to cool completely.

To make the frosting, set a heatproof bowl over a saucepan of barely simmering water, making sure the boiling water does not come into contact with the bottom of the bowl. Pour the cream into the bowl and let it warm slightly. Add the chocolate and cinnamon and stir constantly until the chocolate has melted and the mixture is dark and smooth.

Remove from the heat and let cool for about 30 minutes. Use a palette knife or spatula to spread the frosting evenly over the sides and top of the cake.

60 g/4 tablespoons unsalted butter, at room temperature

50 g/¼ cup light brown soft sugar

1 tablespoon molasses (or black treacle)

2 small eggs, beaten

60 g/½ cup plain/all-purpose flour

1½ teaspoons baking powder

½ teaspoon ground cinnamon

freshly grated zest of 1 orange

50 g/⅓ cup fresh cranberries

20 g/2 tablespoons shelled walnuts, chopped

Sherry-soaked fruits

100 g/⅔ cup raisins

130 g/⅔ cup sultanas/golden raisins

60 g/½ cup mixed peel

3 tablespoons dry sherry

40 ml/3 tablespoons apple juice

Topping

100 g/½ cup apricot jam

100 g/⅔ cup fresh cranberries

80 g/½ cup walnut halves

a 20-cm/8-inch non-stick springform cake tin/pan

Serves 10–12

Cranberry, sherry and vine fruit cake

This is a delicious alternative to traditional Christmas cake. It is loaded with sherry-soaked fruits, walnuts and cranberries.

Prepare the sherry-soaked fruits at least 24 hours in advance. Put the raisins, sultanas/golden raisins, mixed peel, sherry and apple juice in a bowl. Mix, cover and leave to rest for at least 24 hours.

When you are ready to make the cake, preheat the oven to 180°C (350°F) Gas 4.

Put the butter, sugar and molasses in a mixing bowl and mix well. Fold in the eggs, then add the flour, baking powder, cinnamon, orange zest, cranberries and walnuts. Finally, fold in about 190 g/7 oz. of the soaked fruit, setting the rest aside for the topping. Pour the mixture into the prepared baking tin/pan and bake in the preheated oven for 30 minutes, or until deep golden and springy to the touch. Remove from the oven and leave to cool in the tin/pan.

To make the topping, put the apricot jam in a saucepan set over low heat and gently bring to the boil, stirring frequently. Add the cranberries and cook for a few minutes, until their skins just begin to crack. Remove from the heat and stir in the walnuts and the remaining sherry-soaked fruits. Mix well and spoon on top of the cake. Cover the cake evenly and press very slightly to fix it in place. Leave to rest for a few hours before serving.

Birthday cake with cream and berries

4 eggs, at room temperature

225 g/1 cup plus 2 tablespoons caster/granulated sugar

1 teaspoon baking powder

170 g/1⅓ cups self-raising flour

Filling

500 ml/2 cups whipping cream

vanilla sugar or icing/confectioners' sugar, to taste and for dusting (optional)

300 ml/1¼ cups apple juice

your choice of fruit (e.g. berries, sliced bananas, chopped kiwi fruit, canned pineapple chunks)

2 x 26-cm/10-inch springform cake tins/pans, greased

Serves 8–10

This is an old Nordic recipe that oozes with fresh fruit and cream and makes a dazzling alternative to the traditional birthday cake.

Preheat the oven to 200°C (400°F) Gas 6.

Put the eggs and sugar in a large mixing bowl and whisk with a handheld electric whisk until the mixture is foam-like – this will take up to 10 minutes. When it is ready, it will be almost white, have doubled in size and the batter will drop off the beaters in a figure-of-eight when you lift them out of the bowl.

In a separate bowl, sift the baking powder and flour together, then fold into the egg mixture as gently and briefly as possible – do not overwork the mixture otherwise it will lose its fluffiness.

Divide the mixture between the prepared cake tins/pans. Bake in the preheated oven for 35–40 minutes, until the cakes are golden brown and a skewer inserted into the centre of each comes out clean. Leave to cool while you make the filling.

Whip the cream until soft peaks form. Add vanilla sugar or icing/confectioners' sugar to taste, if you like.

Remove the cooled cakes from their tins/pans. Slice each one horizontally through the middle to make two equal layers. Lay one layer on a cake stand. Sprinkle one-quarter of the apple juice evenly over the cake layer. Spread one-quarter of the whipped cream over it, followed by one-quarter of your choice of fruit. Repeat this process four times, finishing with a decorative assortment of fruit on top. Dust lightly with vanilla sugar or icing/confectioners' sugar and serve.

3 chai tea bags

350 g/12 oz. prepared fresh pineapple

250 g/8 oz. mixed soft dried tropical fruit, e.g. pineapple, papaya, mango, melon

100 g/3½ oz. pitted, soft dates

150 g/1 cup raisins

125 g/½ cup dark muscovado or dark brown soft sugar

1 teaspoon bicarbonate of soda/baking soda

1 tablespoon ground allspice

1 teaspoon freshly grated nutmeg

1 small cinnamon stick

3 star anise

4 tablespoons/¼ cup dark rum

150 g/10 tablespoons butter, chopped

grated zest of 2 limes

125 g/1 cup plain/all-purpose flour

125 g/1 cup self-raising flour

100 g/⅔ cup shelled brazil nuts, chopped

2 large eggs, lightly beaten

3 tablespoons runny honey

dried pineapple slices, to decorate

a 20-cm/8-inch cake tin/pan, greased and base-lined with baking parchment

Serves 16

Tropical chai pineapple cake

This soft-textured, moist fruit cake keeps for up to two weeks and is flavoured with chai tea, which has warm undertones of cinnamon and ginger. If you can't find soft dried tropical fruit, use ready-to-eat dried apricots, pears, apples, peaches or prunes, or a mixture, instead.

In a measuring jug/pitcher, make up the tea with 200 ml/¾ cup boiling water. Stir and leave aside while you prepare the rest of the ingredients.

Chop the pineapple into small pieces and set aside.

Chop the dried fruit and the dates into small chunks. Put into a saucepan with the raisins, sugar, bicarbonate of soda/baking soda, all the spices, the rum and butter. Discard the tea bags from the chai tea and pour that into the pan. Stir together and bring the mixture to simmering point over gentle heat.

When the butter has melted, increase the heat and boil the mixture for 2 minutes exactly, then transfer the contents to a large mixing bowl. Stir in the pineapple and lime zest and leave to cool completely, giving it a stir from time to time, as and when you remember.

Preheat the oven to 160°C (325°F) Gas 3.

Remove the cinnamon stick and star anise from the mixture. Sift both flours into the bowl and add the chopped nuts and beaten eggs. Stir well.

Tip the mixture into the prepared tin/pan and spread it evenly with a spatula. Bake in the preheated oven for 1¾ hours, or until risen and deep golden brown. Leave to cool in the tin/pan.

Tip the cold cake out of the tin/pan and peel off the base paper. Warm the honey in a small pan, then use to brush all over the cake. Decorate with dried pineapple slices.

Apple and amaretto cake

450 g/1 lb. dessert apples

350 g/2⅔ cups plain/
all-purpose flour, sifted

1 tablespoon baking powder

2 teaspoons ground cinnamon

200 g/14 tablespoons butter,
softened and cubed

150 g/¾ cup light muscovado
or light brown soft sugar

2 large eggs

100 ml/⅓ cup milk

100 ml/⅓ cup Amaretto

200 g/1⅓ cups sultanas/
golden raisins

To decorate

3 small, red-skinned dessert apples

2 tablespoons runny honey

*a 23-cm/9-inch springform cake
tin/pan, lightly buttered and
base-lined with baking
parchment*

Serves 8–10

*This cake is quick to make and can be left to bake while you get on
with other things. It freezes well and is delicious as is; for added
indulgence, whipped cream mixed with a little sugar and almond-
flavoured Amaretto makes a heavenly accompaniment.*

Preheat the oven to 180°C (350°F) Gas 4.

Core, peel and chop the apples into 1-cm/½-inch chunks.

Tip the flour, baking powder, cinnamon, butter, sugar, eggs, milk and
Amaretto into the bowl of an electric mixer (or use a large mixing bowl
and an electric whisk) and beat together until combined.

Using a large metal spoon, thoroughly stir in the chopped apples and the
sultanas/golden raisins. Spoon the mixture into the prepared tin/pan and
spread it evenly with a spatula.

To decorate, quarter the 3 red-skinned dessert apples. Don't peel them,
but core them and thinly slice the quarters. Arrange the slices, slightly
overlapping, on top of the cake in concentric circles.

Put the tin/pan on a baking sheet and bake in the preheated oven for
1½–1¾ hours, or until risen and golden and the apple slices on top are
burnished. Cover the cake with foil towards the end of cooking to prevent
over-browning, if necessary.

Warm the honey in a small pan, then use to brush over the top of the cake.
Leave to cool in the tin/pan before releasing it, peeling off the base paper
and transferring to a plate or board to slice.

Brownies and Bars

Granola bars

170 g/¾ cup plus 2 tablespoons light brown soft sugar

75 g/⅓ cup golden/corn syrup

130 g/9 tablespoons unsalted butter

75 ml/⅓ cup apple juice

190 g/1 cup jumbo (flaked) oats

190 g/1 cup rolled oats

95 g/¾ cup sultanas/golden raisins

50 g/⅓ cup pumpkin seeds

50 g/⅓ cup sunflower seeds

a 20 x 30-cm/8 x 12-inch baking sheet or tart tin/pan (3 cm/1½ inches deep), lined with baking parchment

Makes 12 large bars

These wholesome, moreish granola bars take almost no time to make and are perfect get-ahead treats for breakfast on the go or a mid-morning snack.

Preheat the oven to 180°C (350°F) Gas 4.

Put the sugar, syrup, butter and apple juice in a saucepan and gently bring to the boil. Remove from the heat and stir in the remaining ingredients until well mixed. Transfer to the prepared tin/pan and spread evenly.

Bake in the preheated oven for 15–20 minutes, then remove from the oven and leave to cool.

Lift the parchment paper, granola and all, up and out of the tin/pan, and transfer to a chopping board. Cut into bars and store in an airtight container for up to 1 week.

Chocolate fudge raspberry shortbread bars

125 g/1 stick butter, at room temperature

50 g/¼ cup granulated sugar

150 g/1 cup plus 2 tablespoons plain/all-purpose flour

Chocolate topping

400 ml/1¾ cups double/heavy cream

2 tablespoons icing/confectioners' sugar

400 g dark/bittersweet chocolate, broken into small pieces

200 g/1½ cups raspberries

a 20-cm/8-inch square tin/pan, ideally loose-based, greased

Makes 21 bars

This is a sophisticated, bite-sized number; the tart fruitiness of the raspberries complements the rich chocolate.

Preheat the oven to 190°C (375°F) Gas 5.

Put the butter and sugar in an electric mixer and beat for 3–4 minutes, or until pale and creamy. Tip in the flour and mix again for a few minutes to combine – the dough probably won't come together in a ball, but if you work it briefly with a wooden spoon and then your hands, it will come together. Tip into the prepared tin/pan and press down firmly with the back of a spoon to make an even layer. Prick the base a few times with a fork. Bake in the preheated oven for 20 minutes, or until lightly golden. Leave to cool.

To make the topping, bring the cream and icing/confectioners' sugar slowly to the boil in a pan. Put the chocolate pieces in a heatproof bowl. As soon as the cream begins to bubble, remove from the heat and pour into the bowl with the chocolate. Gently whisk together until the chocolate has melted and the mixture is smooth.

Stir the raspberries into the chocolate mixture, then pour it over the cooled biscuit base. Leave to cool completely, then refrigerate for 3 hours, or until set. Cut into 21 bars with a sharp knife.

Apple, fig and nut bars

2 large tart apples, such as Granny Smith, peeled, cored and finely chopped

2 tablespoons runny honey

2 tablespoons freshly squeezed orange juice

2 tablespoons apple juice or water

250 g/1½ cups dried figs, finely chopped

375 g/2½ cups plain/all-purpose flour

145 g/1 cup packed light brown soft sugar

250 g/1 stick plus 2 tablespoons unsalted butter, diced

a good pinch of fine sea salt

½ teaspoon ground cinnamon

125 g/1 cup pecans, hazelnuts, walnuts or almonds, finely chopped

a 33 x 23-cm/13 x 9-inch rectangular glass or ceramic baking dish, buttered

Makes 16 bars

These bars fall somewhere between a tart and soft cookie. This filling is slightly reminiscent of fig-centred cookies but the apples make it lighter. Good for brunch, tea time or cake sales, or serve warm with ice cream for dessert.

Preheat the oven to 190°C (375°F) Gas 5.

In a large saucepan, combine the apples, honey, orange and apple juices. Set over low heat, cover and simmer gently, stirring occasionally, until tender, about 10–15 minutes. Use a wooden spoon to help mash the apple pieces. Add the figs and continue simmering, uncovered, until the figs are soft, about 5 minutes. If necessary, add more apple juice or water if the mixture seems too thick, and use a wooden spoon to mash to a coarse purée. Remove from the heat and set aside to cool.

In a food processor, combine the flour, sugar, butter, salt and cinnamon. Pulse to obtain coarse crumbs. Alternatively, blend in a bowl with a pastry cutter, if you have one, or use a palette knife, then rub in using your fingers to obtain coarse crumbs.

Press half the flour mixture into the bottom of the prepared baking dish. Spread the apple and fig mixture over the top in an even layer. Add the nuts to the remaining flour mixture and, using your fingertips, crumble the mixture over the apples in an even layer.

Bake in the preheated oven until browned, about 30–40 minutes. Let cool in the baking dish, then cut into bars. The bars will keep in an airtight container for 7–10 days.

Peanut butter and jam brownies

125 g/4 oz. dark/bittersweet chocolate, chopped

100 g/7 tablespoons butter, diced

175 g/¾ cup plus 1 tablespoon sugar

3 eggs

100 g/¾ cup plus 1 tablespoon plain/all-purpose flour

a pinch of salt

4 generous tablespoons raspberry jam

Peanut butter swirl

75 g/⅓ cup cream cheese

1 egg, lightly beaten

1 teaspoon vanilla extract

100 g/½ cup sugar

150 g/⅔ cup peanut butter

a 20 x 30-cm/8 x 12-inch baking tin/pan, greased and lined with greased baking parchment

Makes 16–20 brownies

Peanut butter and jam are a common sandwich filling, but take away the bread, add some chocolate, swirl it all together and it's a new brownie classic.

Preheat the oven to 170°C (325°F) Gas 3.

Make the peanut butter swirl first. Tip all the ingredients into a bowl and beat until smooth. Set aside.

Put the chocolate and butter in a heatproof bowl set over a saucepan of barely simmering water. Stir until smooth and thoroughly combined. Leave to cool slightly.

In a separate bowl, whisk the sugar and eggs for 2–3 minutes until light and foamy. Add the melted chocolate mixture and stir until combined. Sift the flour and salt into the bowl and fold in until well incorporated.

Spoon two-thirds of the brownie mixture into the prepared baking tin/pan and spread level. Dot one-third of the peanut butter mixture and all of the raspberry jam over the brownie. Spoon over the remaining brownie mixture, then the remaining peanut mixture in equal spoonfuls. Using a round-bladed knife, swirl the mixtures together to create a marbled effect. Tap the tin/pan on the work surface to level the mixture and bake on the middle shelf of the preheated oven for about 20–25 minutes.

Remove from the oven and leave to cool completely in the pan before removing from the tin/pan and cutting into portions to serve.

White chocolate and pecan blondies

Try adding extra interest to these sweet blondies with dried cranberries or a tablespoon of desiccated coconut and swap the pecans for any nut that takes your fancy.

75 g/¾ cup shelled pecans

75 g/2½ oz. white chocolate, chopped

175 g/1½ cups plain/ all-purpose flour

1 teaspoon baking powder

2 tablespoons malted milk powder

a pinch of salt

125 g/1 stick butter, at room temperature

175 g/¾ cup plus 2 tablespoons unrefined sugar

2 eggs, lightly beaten

1 teaspoon vanilla extract

75 g/½ cup white chocolate chips

a 20-cm/8-inch square baking tin/pan, greased and lined with greased baking parchment

Makes 16 blondies

Preheat the oven to 170°C (325°F) Gas 3.

Tip the pecans onto a baking sheet and lightly toast in the preheated oven for 5 minutes. Roughly chop and leave to cool. Leave the oven on for the brownies.

Melt the chocolate either in a heatproof bowl set over a saucepan of barely simmering water or in the microwave on a low setting.

Sift together the flour, baking powder, milk powder and salt.

In a separate bowl, cream together the butter and sugar until pale and light. Gradually add the eggs, beating well after each addition. Stir in the vanilla extract. Add the melted chocolate and stir until combined. Fold the sifted dry ingredients into the bowl until well incorporated, then stir in the chocolate chips and pecans.

Spoon the mixture into the prepared baking tin/pan, spread level and bake on the middle shelf of the preheated oven for 25–30 minutes, or until the brownies are golden and just cooked.

Remove from the oven and leave to cool completely in the tin/pan before removing and cutting into 16 squares to serve.

Rocky roadies

1 quantity Deep Dark Chocolate
brownies (page 98)

75 g/1½ cups mini-marshmallows

75 g/⅔ cup chopped walnuts
or pecans

100 g/3½ oz. glacé cherries
(natural and/or dyed), chopped

100 g/3½ oz. dark/bittersweet
chocolate chips

sugar sprinkles

*a 20 x 30-cm/8 x 12-inch
baking tin/pan, greased and
lined with greased baking
parchment*

Makes 16–20 brownies

*Topped with a mountainous mix of sugary delights –
marshmallows, nuts, cherries and chocolate chips –
here's a combination that's not for the faint-hearted.*

Preheat the oven to 170°C (325°F) Gas 3.

Prepare the Deep Dark Chocolate mixture according to
the recipe on page 98, but bake on the middle shelf of the
preheated oven for just 20 minutes.

Remove from the oven and, working quickly, scatter the
marshmallows, nuts, cherries, chocolate chips and sugar
sprinkles evenly over the top.

Return the brownies to the oven for a further 3 minutes, or
until the marshmallows and chocolate chips are just starting
to melt. Remove from the oven and leave to cool completely
in the tin/pan before cutting into portions to serve.

Coconut, apricot and lime slices

125 g/1 stick butter, softened

50 g/¼ cup demerara sugar

150 g/1 cup plus 2 tablespoons plain/all-purpose flour

450 g/1 lb. ready-to-eat dried apricots, finely chopped

grated zest and freshly squeezed juice of 3 limes

Coconut topping

2 large eggs

1 x 160-ml/5½-oz. can coconut cream

50 g/¼ cup caster/granulated sugar

125 g/1 scant cup desiccated coconut

a 20 x 33-cm/9 x 13-inch baking tin/pan, oiled

Makes 14 slices

These are a modern version of the coconut slice. The traditional version has raspberry jam beneath the coconut topping, but these are all the better for their juicy apricot layer.

Preheat the oven to 180°C (350°F) Gas 4.

Put the butter and sugar in an electric mixer and beat for 3–4 minutes, or until pale and creamy. Add the flour and mix again for a few minutes to combine.

Tip the mixture into the prepared tin/pan and press down firmly with the back of a spoon to make an even layer. Prick the base a few times with a fork. Bake in the preheated oven for 15–20 minutes, or until lightly golden. Leave the oven on.

Meanwhile, put the apricots and lime zest and juice in a medium pan with 60ml/¼ cup cold water and bring to simmering point. Gently cook, covered, for 8–10 minutes, or until soft and mushy. Add another tablespoon of water if the mixture seems too dry as it simmers. Let the apricots cool slightly, then transfer to a food processor and whiz to a thick purée.

To make the coconut topping, lightly beat the eggs in the electric mixer, then add the coconut cream, sugar, and desiccated coconut and mix to combine.

Spread the apricot purée on top of the baked base and top with the coconut mixture, spreading it evenly. Bake for 40–45 minutes, or until golden. Let cool completely before cutting into 14 slices.

Honey, toasted pine nut and pumpkin-seed flapjacks

3 tablespoons pine nuts

2 tablespoons pumpkin seeds

175 g/1½ sticks butter

100 g/½ cup packed light brown soft sugar

3 tablespoons runny honey

100 g/⅔ cup dried sour cherries or cranberries, or chopped ready-to-eat dried apricots, pears, peaches or prunes, or a mixture

250 g/2 cups rolled oats

a pinch of salt

200 g/6½ oz. milk chocolate, broken into pieces

a 20-cm/8-inch square, loose-based tin/pan, lightly buttered

Makes 24 flapjacks

Vary the dried fruit you use in these flapjacks according to what you have handy. They are a hit with children and adults alike.

Preheat the oven to 180°C (350°F) Gas 4.

Spread the pine nuts and pumpkin seeds on a baking sheet and toast in the preheated oven for 5 minutes, or until lightly golden. Leave to cool, then roughly chop.

Gently heat the butter, sugar and honey together in a small saucepan until melted, stirring every now and then. Remove the pan from the heat and leave to cool slightly.

Tip the dried fruit and oats into a large mixing bowl. Add the salt and the chopped pine nuts and seeds. Pour in the warm butter mixture and mix well.

Tip the mixture into the prepared tin/pan and press down firmly with the back of a spoon to make an even layer. Put the tin/pan on a baking sheet. Bake in the preheated oven for 30 minutes, or until lightly golden.

Meanwhile, melt the chocolate in a heatproof bowl set over a pan of barely simmering water. Pour over the flapjack, then leave to cool completely.

Remove the flapjack from the tin/pan and cut into 24 bars.

275 g/9½ oz. dark/bittersweet chocolate, chopped

175 g/1½ sticks butter, diced

125 g/1 cup plain/all-purpose flour

1 teaspoon ground cinnamon

2 teaspoons ground ginger

¼ teaspoon ground nutmeg

a pinch of hot chilli powder

a pinch of salt

50 g/2 oz. crystallized ginger

175 g/¾ cup plus 1 tablespoon dark muscovado/dark brown sugar

2 tablespoons golden/corn syrup

1 tablespoon molasses

4 eggs

50 g/½ cup flaked/slivered almonds, chopped

Chocolate ganache

100g/3½ oz. dark/bittersweet chocolate, finely chopped

150 ml/⅔ cup double/heavy cream

1 tablespoon light brown sugar

a pinch of salt

edible gold sprinkles

a 20-cm/8-inch square baking tin/pan, greased and lined with greased baking parchment

Makes 16 brownies

Gingerbread brownies

These warmly spiced brownies taste even better if you make them a day or two before you plan to serve them – you just have to be patient!

Preheat the oven to 170°C (325°F) Gas 3.

Put the chocolate and butter in a heatproof bowl set over a saucepan of barely simmering water. Stir until smooth and thoroughly combined. Leave to cool slightly.

Sift together the flour, all the spices and the salt. Finely chop the crystallized ginger. Lightly whisk the sugar, syrup, molasses, eggs and vanilla extract until combined. Add the melted chocolate mixture and stir until combined. Stir the almonds and half the chopped ginger into the bowl. Fold in the sifted dry ingredients.

Pour the mixture into the prepared baking tin/pan, spread level and bake on the middle shelf of the preheated oven for about 25 minutes, or until the brownies are set.

Remove from the oven and leave to cool completely in the tin/pan. When cold, remove the brownies from the pan, wrap in clingfilm/plastic wrap and leave overnight before frosting.

The next day, prepare a chocolate ganache by heating the cream and sugar in a small saucepan. Add salt. Pour it over the chopped chocolate and leave to melt. Stir until smooth, then leave to cool. Spread over the top of the brownies, score with the tines of a fork to make a diagonal pattern, then cut into 16 squares. Scatter the rest of the chopped ginger and a few gold sprinkles over the top.

These are brownies in their most simple but decadent form. The little black dress of the brownie world: adorn as you wish.

225 g/8 oz. dark/bittersweet chocolate, chopped

150 g/10 tablespoons butter, diced

125 g/½ cup plus 1 tablespoon sugar

125 g/½ cup plus 1 tablespoon light muscovado/light brown sugar

4 eggs, lightly beaten

1 teaspoon vanilla extract

125 g/1 cup plain/all-purpose flour

a pinch of salt

a 23-cm/9-inch square baking tin/pan, greased and lined with greased baking parchment

Makes 16 brownies

Deep dark chocolate brownies

Preheat the oven to 170°C (325°F) Gas 3.

Put the chocolate and butter in a heatproof bowl set over a saucepan of barely simmering water. Stir until smooth and thoroughly combined. Leave to cool slightly.

Add both the sugars and mix well. Add the eggs one at a time, beating well after each addition. Stir in the vanilla extract. Sift the flour and salt into the bowl and stir until smooth.

Pour the mixture into the prepared baking tin/pan, spread level and bake on the middle shelf of the preheated oven for about 20–25 minutes, or until the brownies are set and have a light crust on top.

Remove from the oven and leave to cool completely in the pan before removing from the pan and cutting into 16 squares to serve.

100 g/¾ cup plain
all-purpose flour

35 g/¼ cup icing/confectioners'
sugar, plus extra for dusting

75 g/5 tablespoons unsalted
butter, chilled and cubed

1–2 figs, very thinly sliced,
to decorate (optional)

Lemon layer

3 large eggs

275 g/1¾ cups granulated sugar

finely grated zest of 1 lemon

150 ml/⅔ cup freshly squeezed
lemon juice (from 3–4 lemons)

50 g/⅓ cup plain/all-purpose
flour, sifted

*an 18-cm/7-inch square
tin/pan, oiled*

Makes 16 squares

Lemon squares

*These look pretty unadorned, lightly dusted with sugar, but
a dainty topping of a slice of fig make them extra special.*

Preheat the oven to 180°C (350°F) Gas 4.

Place 2 wide strips of baking parchment from one side to the other of
the tin/pan so that they form a cross on the base – this will help you
to lift the cake out of the tin/pan when it is cooked. Place a square of
baking parchment on top of the strips, as you would usually do to line
the base of a tin/pan.

Put the flour, icing/confectioners' sugar and butter in an electric mixer
(or use a large mixing bowl and an electric whisk) and whizz until the
mixture resembles breadcrumbs. Tip the mixture into the prepared tin/
pan and press down firmly with the back of a spoon to make an even
layer. Prick the base a few times with a fork. Bake in the preheated
oven for 12–15 minutes, or until lightly golden. Reduce the oven
temperature to 150°C (300°F) Gas 3.

To make the lemon layer, put the eggs, sugar and
lemon zest in the electric mixer and beat for a
minute or so. With the beaters still going, gradually
pour in the lemon juice, then tip in the flour and mix
to combine.

Tip the mixture on top of the baked base. Bake for
45 minutes, by which time the lemon layer will be set
and the top slightly crusty. Leave to cool completely.

Run a sharp knife around the edges, then lift out of the
tin/pan. Lightly dust with icing/confectioners' sugar and cut
into 16 squares. Decorate with the thin slices of fig, if using.

75 g/¾ cup shelled pecans

225 g/1¾ cups plain/
all-purpose flour

1 teaspoon baking powder

½ teaspoon bicarbonate
of soda/baking soda

a pinch of salt

150 g/10 tablespoons soft butter

150 g/¾ cup light brown sugar

100 g/½ cup unrefined sugar

2 eggs, lightly beaten

1 teaspoon vanilla extract

50 g/⅓ cup chocolate chips

75 g/2½ oz. toffees, chopped

To decorate

150 g/¾ cup sugar

150 ml/⅔ cup double/heavy
cream

200 g/1 stick plus 5 tablespoons
soft butter

*a 20 x 30-cm/8 x 12-inch
baking tin/pan, greased and
lined with greased baking
parchment*

*a piping bag, fitted with a
plain nozzle/tip*

Makes 16–20 brownies

Butterscotch brownies

*These are a cross between blondies and brownies, with toffee,
chocolate chips, nuts and caramel frosting. If you can make
spun sugar for decoration, all the better.*

Preheat the oven to 170°C (325°F) Gas 3.

Tip the pecans onto a baking sheet and lightly toast in the preheated
oven for 5 minutes. Roughly chop and leave to cool.

Sift together the flour, baking powder, bicarbonate of soda/baking
soda and salt.

In a separate bowl, cream together the butter and sugars until pale and
light. Gradually add the eggs, beating well after each addition. Stir in
the vanilla extract. Fold the sifted dry ingredients into the bowl until
well incorporated, then stir in the chocolate chips, pecans and toffees.
Spoon the mixture into the prepared baking tin/pan, spread level and
bake on the middle shelf of the preheated oven for 25 minutes.

Remove from the oven and leave to cool completely in the tin/pan.

To decorate, put the sugar and 1 tablespoon water in a small, heavy-
based saucepan over low–medium heat and let the sugar dissolve
without stirring. Raise the heat and continue to cook until the sugar
turns a deep amber colour. Remove from the heat and add the cream
– the caramel will bubble furiously and harden, but stir to melt the
caramel into the cream and leave until completely cold.

Beat the butter until light and fluffy, then add the cold caramel in
a steady stream and stir until thoroughly incorporated and smooth.

Remove the brownies from the tin/pan and cut into portions. Spoon
the caramel frosting into the prepared piping bag and pipe a generous
swirl on top of each brownie.

Hazelnut cheesecake bars

200 g/1½ cups shelled, blanched whole hazelnuts

75 g/5 tablespoons butter

200 g/6½ oz. ginger nut biscuits/gingersnaps, broken into pieces

icing/confectioners' sugar, for dusting

Cheesecake topping

400 g/14 oz. cream cheese

175 g/¾ cup caster/granulated sugar

3 large eggs

300 ml/1¾ cups sour cream

a 20 x 33-cm/9 x 13-inch baking tin/pan, oiled

Makes 14 bars

These bars will keep in the fridge for a day or so. They are ideal for coffee time or they also double up well as a simple dessert with poached fruit alongside.

Preheat the oven to 180°C (350°F) Gas 4.

Spread the hazelnuts on a baking sheet and toast in the preheated oven for 10–12 minutes, then leave to cool. Reduce the oven temperature to 160°C (325°F) Gas 3.

Melt the butter in a small pan and leave to cool slightly.

Tip the biscuits/snaps into a food processor. Add half the cooled hazelnuts and whizz together until you have fine crumbs. Add the melted butter and briefly whizz again. Tip the mixture into the prepared baking tin/pan and press down firmly with the back of a spoon to make an even layer. Put the tin/pan on a baking sheet.

To make the cheesecake topping, put all the ingredients in an electric mixer (or use a large mixing bowl and an electric whisk) and whisk to combine. Carefully pour the mixture on top of the biscuit base in the tin/pan – the mixture will come pretty near the top. Roughly chop the remaining hazelnuts and scatter over the cheesecake. Bake in the preheated oven for 45 minutes. Leave to cool completely.

Refrigerate for 30 minutes before cutting into 14 bars with a sharp knife. The cheesecake will be soft-set. Lightly dust with icing/confectioners' sugar.

Coconut and pumpkin power bars

100 g/7 tablespoons butter

50 g/¼ cup extra virgin coconut oil

150 g/¾ cup caster/granulated sugar

3 tablespoons golden/light corn syrup

80 g/¾ cup self-raising flour

2 eggs, beaten

150 g/2 cups desiccated coconut

100 g/1 cup shelled unsalted pistachios

60 g/½ cup pumpkin seeds

60 g/½ cup sunflower seeds

60 g/½ cup pine nuts

150 g/1 cup raisins or sultanas/golden raisins

a 30 x 20-cm/12 x 8-inch deep-sided baking tin/pan, greased and base-lined

Makes 14 bars

These hearty bars, packed with nuts, seeds and dried fruit, are perfect for a quick energy fix. They are ideal for lunchboxes, mid-morning snacks or as after-school treats. But even though they contain plenty of natural goodness, they are still a treat for your tastebuds and will keep your tummy happy between meals.

Preheat the oven to 180°C (350°F) Gas 4.

Put the butter, coconut oil, sugar and syrup in a large saucepan and heat until the butter has melted. Take off the heat and leave to cool slightly.

Sift the flour into a mixing bowl and add all the remaining ingredients. Stir with a wooden spoon until everything is well mixed together. Pour in the cooled butter mixture and mix together.

Tip the mixture into the prepared tin/pan and press down using the back of a spoon. Bake in the preheated oven for 20–25 minutes, until the top is golden brown and the mixture feels firm to the touch. Let cool completely in the tin/pan then tip out onto a chopping board and cut into bars to serve.

These bars will keep for up to 5 days if stored in an airtight container.

Ginger marble cake bars

These ginger cake bars are the height of luxury. They look incredibly sophisticated but serve beautifully as an indulgent treat. A perfect accompaniment to a strong espresso.

150 g/6 oz. ginger biscuits/
old-fashioned gingersnaps

125 g/1 stick unsalted butter

200 g/7 oz. dark chocolate,
broken into pieces

1 tablespoon golden caster/
superfine sugar

2 tablespoons golden/corn syrup

50 g/⅓ cup chopped crystallized
ginger

Topping

200 g/7 oz. dark chocolate,
chopped

50 g/2 oz. milk chocolate,
chopped

*an 18 x 28-cm/11 x 7-inch
Swiss roll tin/jelly roll pan,
lined with foil*

Makes 12 bars

Crush the biscuits/snaps into small pieces. The easiest way to do this is to put them in a polythene bag and bash with a rolling pin, but not too much as you do want pieces not crumbs.

Put the butter, dark chocolate, sugar and golden/corn syrup in a large heavy-based saucepan and set over low heat. Let melt, stirring continuously.

Take off the heat, add the crushed biscuits/snaps and ginger and mix well until everything is coated in the chocolate mixture. Pour the mixture into the prepared tin/pan and transfer to the fridge to set.

To make the topping, melt the dark chocolate in a bowl set over a saucepan of barely simmering water. Pour the chocolate over the chilled mixture, spreading it over the surface with a metal spatula. Return to the fridge to set before decorating.

To decorate, melt the milk chocolate in a heatproof bowl set over a saucepan of barely simmering water. When just melted remove the bowl from the heat. Dip the tines of a fork into the melted chocolate and holding it above the marble cake, move it backwards and forwards to drizzle the chocolate in a random pattern over the top.

Return to the fridge to set the milk chocolate and then cut into bars with a hot knife.

Breads, Buns and Scones

Scones with strawberry jam and plenty of clotted cream

1 large egg

about 125 ml/½ cup milk

a squeeze of lemon juice

225 g/1¾ cups plain/all-purpose flour

2 rounded teaspoons baking powder

2 tablespoons caster/granulated sugar, plus extra for sprinkling

a pinch of salt

50 g/3 tablespoons butter, softened and cubed

strawberry jam, to serve

clotted cream, to serve

a plain 5-cm/2-inch cookie cutter

a baking sheet, oiled

Makes about 10 scones

Scones are best eaten the day they are made, but they do freeze well if you have a few left over. Another time, try adding the grated zest of a lemon and a small handful of sultanas or chopped, pitted dates to the mix.

Preheat the oven to 220°C (425°F) Gas 7.

Put the egg and milk in a small jug/pitcher and lightly beat, then mix in the lemon juice.

Sift the flour and baking powder into a large mixing bowl and stir in the 2 tablespoons of sugar and the salt.

Scatter the cubes of butter over the flour mixture and, using a table knife, cut them into the flour. Now, lightly rub the butter into the flour, using your fingertips, until the mixture resembles breadcrumbs.

Pour in half the egg mixture and, using the knife again, mix the liquid into the dry ingredients using a cutting action. Add as much of the remaining egg mixture as you need to, to be able to bring everything together into a dough – you probably won't need it all.

Tip the dough out onto a lightly floured work surface and gently pat it out until it is about 2.5 cm/1 inch thick. Using the cookie cutter, stamp out scones, then gently re-form the dough and continue until you have used it all.

Arrange the scones on the baking sheet. Brush the tops with any leftover egg mixture and sprinkle with caster/granulated sugar. Bake in the preheated oven for 10–12 minutes, or until risen and golden.

Easy banana bread

200 g/¾ cup golden caster/
granulated sugar

2 eggs

125 ml/½ cup pure vegetable oil

2 bananas, peeled and mashed

260 g/2 cups plain wholemeal/
whole-wheat flour

1½ teaspoons baking powder

1 teaspoon ground cinnamon

fresh ricotta and honey, to serve
(optional)

*a 20 x 10 cm/8 x 4 inch loaf
tin/pan, greased*

Makes 1 medium loaf

*This is the simplest of bread recipes. Make it on the morning
you intend to eat it and fill the house with the seductive
smell of cinnamon. Serve it warm spread with fresh ricotta
and honey. Or make it a day or two in advance and lightly
toast to serve.*

Preheat the oven to 180°C (350°F) Gas 4.

Whisk the sugar and eggs together in a bowl. Stir in the oil and
65 ml/¼ cup cold water until well combined.

Stir in the mashed bananas, flour, baking powder and cinnamon
until just combined. Spoon into the prepared loaf tin/pan and
bake in the preheated oven for 50–55 minutes, until golden and
firm on top. Let cool in the tin/pan for 10 minutes before inverting
onto a wire rack.

Serve warm on the day it is made or cooled and toasted, with
ricotta and honey, if liked. The bread will keep for up to 2 days
in an airtight container.

Variation: For a tasty banana and date bread, add 100 g/3½ oz.
chopped pitted dates to the mixture. This mixture also makes
great muffins – just spoon the mixture into a greased 12-hole
muffin tin/pan and bake in a preheated oven at 180°C (350°F)
Gas 4 for 20–25 minutes, until risen and golden. Drizzle over
a little honey while the muffins are still warm.

Apple and carrot bread with walnuts

250 g/1¾ cups plain/all-purpose flour

150 g/¾ cup light muscovado/light brown soft sugar

1 tablespoon baking powder

a pinch of sea salt

1 teaspoon ground cinnamon

½ teaspoon ground nutmeg

¼ teaspoon each ground ginger and allspice

100 ml/⅔ cup apple juice

75 g/5 tablespoons unsalted butter, melted

2 large eggs, beaten

1 large tart cooking apple, such as Bramley's or Granny Smith, peeled, cored and grated

100 g/1 cup grated carrots

65 g/½ cup walnuts, coarsely chopped

a 900-g/2-lb. loaf tin/pan, buttered

Serves 6–8

This tasty and enriching loaf goes a long way and keeps well for a few days. It is very nice plain, or spread with butter or cream cheese for something more substantial. The smell of freshly baked nutty bread wafting through the house is worth the effort alone.

Preheat the oven to 180°C (350°F) Gas 4.

In a mixing bowl, combine the flour, sugar, baking powder, salt, cinnamon, nutmeg, ginger and allspice. Set aside.

In a separate bowl, mix together the apple juice, melted butter and eggs. Gently fold this mixture into the flour mixture to combine. Use your hands to squeeze every last drop of moisture from the grated apple and carrots then add to the mixture, along with the walnuts and stir just to combine.

Transfer the mixture to the prepared loaf tin/pan and level the top. Bake in the preheated oven until a skewer inserted in the centre of the bread comes out clean, about 1–1¼ hours.

Leave the bread to cool in the tin/pan for a few minutes then turn out onto a wire rack to cool completely. Slice to serve. The bread will keep in an airtight container for 4–5 days.

Swedish saffron buns

These buns are traditionally served on St Lucy's day in Sweden, 13th December, where they call them 'lussekatt'. They are normally made into a backwards 'S' shape, but can be made into any shape you like.

250 ml/1 cup milk

a good pinch of saffron strands

500–600 g/4–4¾ cups strong white/bread flour

1 x 7-g/¼-oz. sachet easy-blend dried yeast

½ teaspoon salt

50 g/¼ cup caster/granulated sugar

50 g/3 tablespoons unsalted butter, at room temperature

100 ml/⅓ cup sour cream, at room temperature

1 egg, lightly beaten

24 raisins

2 baking sheets, lined with baking parchment

Makes 12 buns

Heat the milk in a small saucepan until hot but not boiling. Add the saffron and leave to infuse in the hot milk for 10 minutes.

Tip 500 g/4 cups of the flour, the yeast, salt, sugar, butter and sour cream into a large mixing bowl and stir to mix. Pour the warm milk in and use your hands to mix everything together until you get a dough.

Knead the dough, then shape the dough into a ball and push on it and press it onto the work surface, turning it round often. Keep doing this until it is silky smooth and elastic – this will take between 4–7 minutes and you may need to add more flour if the dough is too sticky. Shape the dough into a neat ball again. Wash and dry the mixing bowl and sit the dough back in it. Cover tightly with clingfilm/plastic wrap and leave in a warm place until the dough has doubled in size. This can take at least 1 hour.

Tip the dough onto the floured work surface and knead for 1 minute. Divide into 12 equal pieces. Roll each piece into a 20-cm/8-inch long sausage and twist into a backwards 'S' shape. Place the buns on the baking sheets. Cover the sheets with a lightly oiled sheet of clingfilm/plastic wrap. Leave the buns to rise again for a further 30 minutes.

Preheat the oven to 190°C (375°F) Gas 5. Brush the buns lightly with the beaten egg and push a raisin into each end of the buns. Bake for about 12–15 minutes, until well risen, shiny and deep golden brown.

These are filled with a sugary cinnamon butter and topped with a crazy drizzle of icing. Add chocolate chips to the filling for an extra helping of sweetness!

Cinnamon sticky buns

Heat the milk in a small saucepan until hot but not boiling. Sift 500 g/ 4 cups of the flour into a large mixing bowl and stir in the yeast, salt and sugar. Make a hole like a well in the middle and pour in the warm milk, eggs and butter. Stir until mixed.

Knead the dough until it is silky smooth and elastic – about 5 minutes – and you may need to add more flour if the dough is too sticky. Shape the dough into a neat ball again. Wash and dry the mixing bowl and sit the dough back in it. Cover tightly with clingfilm/plastic wrap and leave in a warm place until the dough has doubled in size. This will take about 1½ hours.

To make the filling, put the butter, sugar, cinnamon and pecans in a bowl. Beat with a wooden spoon until mixed.

Tip the dough onto the floured work surface and knead lightly for 1 minute. Roll and press it into a rectangle about 30 x 50 cm/12 x 20 inches, with a long side nearest you. Spread the filling over the dough, leaving a border of about 1 cm/½ inch around the edges. Roll the dough up evenly and firmly, but not too tight. Cut into 12 slices and place cut-side up in the baking tin/pan. Cover the baking tin/pan and leave in a warm place for 30 minutes, or until risen.

Preheat the oven to 180°C (350°F) Gas 4. Bake for 30–35 minutes until golden brown. Remove the tin/pan from the oven and leave it to cool completely.

Sift the icing/confectioners' sugar into a bowl and gradually stir in enough water to make a smooth icing. Using a spoon, drizzle the icing over the buns. Leave to set before tipping them out of the tin/pan and pulling them apart, to serve.

150 ml/⅔ cup milk

500–600 g/4–4¾ cups strong white/bread flour

1 x 7-g/¼-oz. sachet easy-blend dried yeast

a large pinch of salt

50 g/¼ cup caster/granulated sugar

2 eggs, lightly beaten

75 g/5 tablespoons unsalted butter, at room temperature

250g/2 cups icing/ confectioners' sugar

Filling

100 g/6 tablespoons unsalted butter, at room temperature

100 g/½ cup light brown soft sugar

3 teaspoons ground cinnamon

75 g/½ cup pecan pieces

a 23 x 30-cm/9 x 12-inch baking tin/pan, greased

Makes 12 buns

Cherry berry buns

This is a really quick and easy recipe. The buns are packed with a mixture of dried fruit – cherries, cranberries, strawberries and blueberries. You'll find bags of these mixed dried 'berries and cherries' in supermarkets and wholefood stores, or you can also use jumbo raisins or why not make up your own combination?

250 g/2 cups plain/
all-purpose flour

4 teaspoons baking powder

¼ teaspoon ground mixed/
apple pie spice

100 g/7 tablespoons unsalted
butter, at room temperature

50 g/⅓ cup light muscovado/
light brown soft sugar

125 g/1 cup cherry berry mix
(see above)

1 large free-range egg

5 tablespoons milk

caster/granulated or demerara
sugar, for sprinkling

*2 non-stick baking sheets,
lightly greased*

Makes 18 small buns

Preheat the oven to 200°C (400°F) Gas 6.

Sift the flour, baking powder and mixed/apple pie spice into a large mixing bowl. Cut the butter into small pieces and add to the bowl. Work the butter into the flour by rubbing it in with the tips of your fingers until the mixture looks like breadcrumbs. Stir in the muscovado/light brown sugar and cherry berry mix and make a well in the mixture.

Break the egg into a small bowl, add the milk and beat the mixture with a fork just to break up the egg and mix it with the milk. Pour into the well in the flour mixture and mix all the ingredients together with a round-bladed knife to make a firm dough. If there are dry crumbs or the dough won't mix together add another tablespoon of milk.

Drop spoonfuls of the mixture on to the prepared baking sheets, using about a generous tablespoon of mixture for each bun, spacing them slightly apart. Sprinkle each bun with a little sugar and bake in the preheated oven to bake for 15 minutes, until golden brown. Remove the sheets from the oven and leave to cool for 2 minutes. Transfer the buns to a wire rack to cool completely. Store your buns in an airtight container and eat them within 3 days.

Apple and sultana scones

225 g/1¾ cups plain/
all-purpose flour

4 teaspoons baking powder

2 tablespoons caster/
granulated sugar

50 g/3 tablespoons unsalted
butter, chilled and diced

1 apple, peeled, cored
and finely diced

40 g/⅓ cup sultanas/
golden raisins

1 egg

80 ml/5 tablespoons milk

crème fraîche, to serve

good-quality lemon curd,
to serve

*a plain 5-cm/2-inch cookie
cutter*

a baking sheet, greased

Makes about 12 scones

*Crème fraîche and lemon curd make the perfect additions to
these light and fruity scones. The tiny chunks of apple in the
dough retain a crisp bite, giving the scones a lovely texture
and moistness.*

Put the flour, baking powder and sugar in a food processor and pulse
to combine. Add the butter and process for about 20 seconds until the
mixture resembles fine breadcrumbs. Transfer to a large bowl, stir in
the apple and sultanas/golden raisins, then make a well in the centre
of the mixture.

Beat together the egg and milk in another bowl, reserving 1 tablespoon
of the mixture in a separate bowl. Pour most of the remaining liquid
into the flour mixture and bring together into a soft dough using a
fork. If there are still dry crumbs, add a little more of the liquid. Turn
out onto a lightly floured surface and knead briefly until smooth.
Gently pat or roll out the dough to about 2.5 cm/1 inch thick. Cut out
rounds with the cookie cutter, pressing the trimmings together to
make more scones.

Arrange the scones on the prepared baking sheet, spacing them
slightly apart. Brush the tops with the reserved egg and milk mixture
and bake in preheated oven at 220°C (425°F) Gas 7 for 10–12 minutes
until risen and golden. Transfer to a wire rack to cool slightly. Serve
warm with crème fraîche and lemon curd.

Toasted teacakes

There's something particularly comforting and homely about a plateful of freshly toasted teacakes dripping with butter, and the wonderful smell of spices that they always emit. If you've got an old-fashioned toasting fork with a long handle, why not toast the teacakes the traditional way over the open fire.

225 g/1½ cups strong white/
bread flour

½ teaspoon sea salt

1 teaspoon easy-blend
dried yeast

15 g/1½ tablespoons light brown
soft sugar

¼ teaspoon freshly grated nutmeg

60 g/⅓ cup mixed dried
vine fruits

40 g/3 tablespoons butter,
melted

120 ml/½ cup whole milk,
plus extra for brushing

butter, to serve

Makes 8 teacakes

Sift the flour, salt, yeast, sugar and nutmeg into a large bowl. Stir in the dried fruits and make a well in the centre.

Put the milk and butter in a small saucepan and heat together until just warm. Pour into the flour mixture and gradually work together to make a soft dough. Turn out on to a lightly floured work surface and knead for about 5 minutes, until smooth and elastic. Place in a bowl, slip the bowl into a large plastic bag, seal with a rubber band and leave to rise for 1 hour, until doubled in size. When risen, tip the dough out on to a lightly floured work surface, punch down, and divide into eight pieces of equal size. Shape each one into a ball, flatten slightly and arrange on a greased baking sheet, spacing slightly apart. Slip the sheet into a large plastic bag and leave the dough to rise again for 45 minutes, until doubled in size.

Preheat the oven to 200°C (400°F) Gas 6. Brush the top of each teacake with milk, then bake for about 15 minutes, until risen and golden and sounds hollow when the base is gently tapped. Transfer to a wire rack to cool. When ready to serve, split, toast on the cut sides and spread generously with butter.

115 g/1 stick butter

170 g/½ cup black treacle/molasses

60 g/scant ¼ cup golden/light corn syrup

30 g/2 tablespoons dark brown soft sugar

125 ml/½ cup milk

2 eggs

115 g/¾ cup plus 1 tablespoon plain/all-purpose baking flour

115 g/1 cup ground almonds

1 teaspoon mixed/apple pie spice

1 teaspoon ground cinnamon

2 teaspoons ground ginger

1 teaspoon bicarbonate of soda/baking soda

1 teaspoon vanilla extract

finely grated zest of 2 small oranges

1 large apple, cored and grated

50 g/⅓ cup flaked/slivered almonds

icing/confectioners' sugar, for dusting

a 35 x 25-cm/14 x 10-inch cake tin/pan, greased and base-lined

Makes 16 squares

Apple and orange gingerbread

The comforting smell of gingerbread makes any visitor feel welcome. This is how gingerbread should be – dark, sticky and laden with treacle – but with the added zesty twist of apple and orange. Perfect with a cup of tea and, failing a visitor, a good book.

Preheat the oven to 180°C (350°F) Gas 4.

Put the butter, treacle/molasses, syrup and sugar in a saucepan and heat gently until the butter has melted and the sugar dissolved. Whisk in the milk, set aside to cool for 10 minutes then beat in the eggs.

Sift the flour into a mixing bowl and stir in the ground almonds, spices, bicarbonate of soda/baking soda, vanilla, orange zest, apple and almonds.

Pour the treacle mixture into the dry ingredients and mix well. Pour the batter into the prepared tin/pan and bake in the preheated oven for 30–40 minutes, until the gingerbread is firm to touch but still soft. Remove from the oven and let cool in the tin/pan. Dust with icing/confectioners' sugar and cut into squares to serve.

This gingerbread will keep for up to 3 days if stored in an airtight container.

Pear and blackberry scone round

225 g/1¾ cups self-raising flour
plus 1 teaspoon baking powder

200 g/2 cups ground almonds

2 teaspoons ground cinnamon

½ teaspoon fine sea salt

115 g/1 stick butter, chilled
and cubed

55 g/¼ cup caster/granulated
sugar, plus extra for sprinkling

200 ml/¾ cup buttermilk

200 g/1 cup blackberries

2 ripe pears, peeled, cored
and sliced

1 egg, beaten

*a baking sheet, greased
and lined*

Makes 8 slices

*This delicious recipe uses ripe blackberries with seasonal pears
for a rustic scone that's perfect served warm with plenty of
creamy butter. A lovely autumnal treat for tea with friends.*

Preheat the oven to 190°C (375°C) Gas 5.

Put the flour, baking powder, ground almonds, cinnamon and salt in
a large mixing bowl and stir together.

Add the butter and rub into the flour with your fingertips, until the
mixture resembles fine breadcrumbs. Add the sugar and buttermilk and
mix to form a soft dough, adding a little milk if the mixture is too dry.
Add the blackberries and pear slices and gently bring the dough
together with your hands.

Put the dough on a floured work surface and shape it into a 23-cm/
9-inch diameter round. Transfer to the prepared baking sheet using a
large spatula. Brush the scone round with the beaten egg and sprinkle
with a little extra sugar. Using a sharp knife, score the top of the scone
into 8 sections but do not cut all the way through the dough. Bake in
the preheated oven for 20–25 minutes, until golden brown and the
scone sounds hollow when you tap it. Serve warm with butter.

This scone round is best eaten on the day it is made.

Honey buns

60 g/5 tablespoons butter

50 g/¼ cup caster/
superfine sugar

4 tablespoons clear honey

80 ml/⅓ cup full-fat milk

1 egg, beaten

115 g/¾ cup self-raising flour

To decorate

200 g/1¾ cups icing/
confectioners' sugar, sifted

2 tablespoons freshly squeezed
lemon juice

assorted coloured sprinkles

*a 12-hole cupcake tin/pan,
lined with paper cases*

Makes 12 buns

*These sticky little cakes are the perfect treat to make for the
honey bun or buns in your life. Nibble on them with a cup
of tea and they'll add a little sparkle to your day.*

Preheat the oven to 170°C (325°F) Gas 3.

Put the butter, sugar and honey in a saucepan and warm gently,
stirring constantly, until the butter has melted. Remove the pan
from the heat and stir in the milk. Stir in the egg, then sift in the
flour and mix together.

Spoon the mixture into the paper cases and bake in the preheated
oven for about 20 minutes, until golden and risen. Leave the cakes
to cool in the tin/pan for a couple of minutes, then transfer to a
wire rack to cool completely.

To decorate, stir the lemon juice into the icing/confectioners' sugar
until you have a thick, spoonable consistency. If necessary, add a
little more lemon juice. Spoon the icing on to the cakes and finish
with coloured sprinkles. Let set before serving.

a wine-mulling spice bag

200 ml/¾ cup light, fruity red wine

1 tablespoon runny honey

75 g/½ cup ready-to-eat dried figs

50 g/⅓ cup crystallized stem ginger

75 g/⅓ cup whole blanched almonds

50 g/⅓ cup each dried cranberries and dried sour cherries (or use 100 g/⅔ cup sultanas/golden raisins)

100 g/½ cup light muscovado or light brown soft sugar

2 large eggs, lightly beaten

grated zest of 2 oranges

100 g/1 cup fresh cranberries

225 g/1¾ cups self-raising flour

1 teaspoon ground cinnamon

½ teaspoon ground allspice

Topping

75 g/½ cup dried cranberries (or dried sour cherries, or sultanas/golden raisins)

2 tablespoons freshly squeezed orange juice

4 tablespoons/¼ cup redcurrant jelly

a 19 x 9-cm/8½ x 4½-inch loaf tin/pan, lightly buttered and base-lined with baking parchment

Serves 12

Mulled wine and cranberry tea bread

This loaf is studded with juicy fruit and nuts, perfect for autumn and winter. It is delicious sliced and eaten as it is or spread with unsalted butter.

First make the mulled wine. Put the wine-mulling spice bag in a saucepan with the red wine and honey. Slowly bring to a simmer, stirring now and then. Leave over very low heat for 5 minutes, then take the pan off the heat and set aside.

Roughly chop the figs, ginger and almonds and mix with the dried cranberries and cherries and the sugar in a mixing bowl. Remove the spice bag from the mulled wine, then pour the warm wine over the dried fruit and leave to soak for 30 minutes.

Preheat the oven to 160°C (325°F) Gas 3.

Stir the beaten eggs, orange zest and the fresh cranberries into the soaked dried fruit. Next, sift in the flour, cinnamon and allspice. Mix together until thoroughly combined.

Spoon the mixture into the prepared loaf tin/pan. Bake in the preheated oven for 55 minutes, by which time the loaf will have risen and slightly shrunk from the sides of the tin/pan. Leave to cool in the tin/pan, then run a table knife around the edge of the tin/pan, tip the loaf out and peel off the base paper.

To make the topping, gently heat the cranberries, orange juice and redcurrant jelly in a small pan over low heat, stirring until the jelly has dissolved.

Brush the top of the loaf with some of the sticky juices from the topping, then spoon the cranberries along the centre of the loaf. Leave to cool before serving.

Crunchy prune and vanilla custard brioche cakes

2 large eggs

2 tablespoons Armagnac or other brandy

4 tablespoons demerara sugar

250 g thick ready-made custard and ½ teaspoon vanilla extract OR
2 x 4-oz. vanilla pudding snack cups

75 g/5 tablespoons butter

200 g/6½ oz. brioche

100 g/⅔ cup pitted, soft Agen prunes, snipped into small pieces

a 6-hole muffin tin/pan, each hole well buttered and lined with a 17-cm/7-inch square of baking parchment

Makes 6 cakes

These individual cakes have an indulgent fruity custard hiding under their crunchy topping. They are also good made with limoncello instead of the brandy, but leave out the alcohol altogether if you prefer. Use the thick custard you can buy in cartons from the supermarket, and if time is really short, use muffin cases instead of making your own liners. These are best eaten on the day they are made.

Preheat the oven to 180°C (350°F) Gas 4.

In a mixing bowl and using a balloon whisk, whisk together the eggs, Armagnac, 1 tablespoon of the sugar, the vanilla and the custard/vanilla pudding cups.

Melt the butter in a small pan and pour into a large mixing bowl.

Cut the brioche into 1–1½-cm/½-inch squares. Toss the squares in the melted butter with 2 tablespoons of the sugar, mixing well. Divide half the squares between the parchment-lined holes in the muffin tin/pan, pressing them down firmly to make a base.

Divide the prune pieces between each muffin, then do the same with the egg mixture. Now add the rest of the brioche squares to the muffins, piling it up high. Scatter the remaining sugar over the top.

Bake in the preheated oven for 35 minutes, or until set and golden on top. Eat warm or cold.

Biscuits and Cookies

Fig, apricot and nut biscotti

200 g/1½ cups plain/
all-purpose flour

1½ teaspoons baking powder

100 g/½ cup golden caster/
granulated sugar

30 g/¼ cup shelled
pistachio nuts

30 g/¼ cup shelled hazelnuts

30 g/¼ cup sultanas/
golden raisins

40 g/4 dried apricots, quartered

40 g/4 dried figs, quartered

freshly grated zest of 1 small
lemon

2 eggs, lightly beaten

*a baking sheet, lined with
baking parchment*

Makes about 28 biscotti

*These double-baked crisp biscotti are packed with dried
fruit and nuts, and are made lighter without butter. They
are best enjoyed with a cup of strong coffee or dipped in
some vanilla ice cream for a sweet treat.*

Preheat the oven to 150°C (300°F) Gas 2.

Sift the flour and baking powder into a mixing bowl. Stir in the
sugar, pistachio nuts, hazelnuts, sultanas/golden raisins, apricots,
figs and lemon zest.

Pour in the eggs and mix well until you get a dough-like mixture.
Bring the dough together into a ball in your hands and transfer
it to the prepared baking sheet.

Flour your hands and roll the dough into a log (you can use the
parchment paper to help you roll the dough). Flatten it slightly
so that it is about 8 cm/3 inches wide.

Bake in the preheated oven for about 30 minutes. To check if it's
ready, press very lightly on top of the log and if it springs back
you can take it out of the oven. If it still feels very firm, leave it in
the oven for a few more minutes. When it is ready, remove from
the oven and leave to cool for about 10 minutes.

Using a large, serrated bread knife, slice the log into 5-mm/¼-inch
slices. Lay the slices on the baking sheet and return to the hot
oven for 10 minutes, turning them halfway through cooking.
When they are pale gold, remove from the oven and leave to cool
for a few minutes. Store in an airtight container for up to 2 weeks.

150 g/1 cup plus 2 tablespoons
plain/all-purpose flour

1 teaspoon baking powder

15 g/1½ tablespoons cocoa powder

50 g/¼ cup light brown soft sugar

65 g/4 tablespoons unsalted butter,
chilled and cubed

45 g/2½ tablespoons runny honey

1 teaspoon water

To decorate

100 g/3½ oz. white chocolate,
chopped

30 g/¼ cup shelled almonds, chopped

30 g/¼ cup shelled pistachio nuts,
chopped

30 g/¼ cup shelled pecan nuts,
chopped (optional)

30 g/¼ cup dried cranberries,
chopped

*an 11-cm/4-inch high,
egg-shaped cookie cutter*

*a baking sheet, lined with
baking parchment*

Makes 5 biscuits

Easter egg biscuits

*These are fabulous looking chocolate biscuits, studded like
jewels with dried fruit and nuts. You can decorate them by
scattering the nuts and dried fruit over them haphazardly
or spend time over an artistic design. Either way, they make
thoughtful Easter gifts.*

Preheat the oven to 170°C (325°F) Gas 3.

Put the flour, baking powder, cocoa, sugar, butter and honey in
a food processor and pulse until you get crumbs. Add the water
and mix until a smooth ball of dough has formed.

Transfer the dough to a lightly floured surface and roll out with
a rolling pin until about 5 mm/¼ inch thick. Cut out egg shapes
with the cookie cutter and place on the prepared baking sheet.

Bake in the preheated oven for 25 minutes, then leave to cool
before decorating.

To decorate, put the chocolate in a heatproof bowl set over a
saucepan of barely simmering water. Do not let the base of the
bowl touch the water. Stir until melted.

Brush the melted chocolate over one side of each biscuit with
a pastry brush, then scatter the nuts and cranberries over the
top. If you prefer, you can arrange the decoration in a pattern.

Leave the chocolate to cool and set before serving. Store in an
airtight container away from sunlight for up to 2 weeks.

Passion-fruit sandwiches

500 g/4 sticks butter, softened

100 g/⅔ cup icing/confectioners' sugar, sifted, plus extra for dusting

400 g/3⅓ cups plain/all-purpose flour, sifted

100 g/¾ cup cornflour/cornstarch, sifted

Passion-fruit cream

100 g/6 tablespoons mascarpone

75 g/½ cup icing/confectioners' sugar, sifted

pulp of 2 passion fruit

a piping bag, fitted with a wide plain or star nozzle/tip

3 baking sheets, lined with baking parchment

Makes 14 biscuits

These are dainty, melt-in-the-mouth biscuits sandwiched together with a passion-fruit cream. Choose passion fruit that have wrinkled skins, as they will be the most fragrant and juicy.

Preheat the oven to 180°C (350°F) Gas 4.

Put the butter and sugar in an electric mixer (or use a large mixing bowl and an electric whisk) and beat together until pale and creamy. Tip in the flour and cornflour/cornstarch and whisk again to combine.

Fill the piping bag with the mixture and use to pipe 9-cm/3½-inch lengths onto the prepared baking sheets. Leave room between them to allow the biscuits to spread as they bake. Bake in the preheated oven for 15–18 minutes, or until lightly golden at the edges. Leave to cool on the baking sheets.

To make the passion-fruit cream, mix all the ingredients together and refrigerate until needed.

Sandwich the biscuits together with the passion-fruit cream and lightly dust the top of each sandwich with icing/confectioners' sugar.

Applesauce cookies

50 g/5 tablespoons unsalted
butter, at room temperature

100 g/½ cup light brown
soft sugar

180 g/¼ cup jarred apple sauce

150 g/1 cup plain/
all-purpose flour

½ teaspoon bicarbonate
of soda/baking soda

½ teaspoon baking powder

½ teaspoon ground cinnamon

a pinch of fine sea salt

50 g/½ cup raisins or sultanas/
golden raisins

45 g/½ cup chopped nuts, such
as walnuts or pecans

*a baking sheet, lined with
baking parchment*

Makes 10–12 cookies

*Apples, raisins and cinnamon are a magical combination. In
these cookies they bring out the very best in each other and make
for a juicy and chewy teatime treat.*

Preheat the oven to 200°C (400°F) Gas 6.

Put the butter and sugar in a mixing bowl and beat together with a
hand-held electric whisk until light and fluffy. Stir in the apple sauce.

In a separate bowl, combine the flour, bicarbonate of soda/baking
soda, baking powder, cinnamon and salt and mix well. Add the dry
ingredients to the butter mixture and blend well using a wooden
spoon. Add the sultanas/golden raisins and nuts and fold in.

Drop walnut-sized spoonfuls of the mixture at even intervals onto the
prepared baking sheet. Bake in the preheated oven until the cookies
are just golden around the edges but still soft, about 12–15 minutes.
Transfer to a wire rack to cool. Continue baking in batches until all
the mixture has been used.

The cookies can be stored in an airtight container for up to 4 days.

These little Italian biscuits are pronounced 'reech-ee-a-relly'. They're chewy and sticky and yummy. Dust them in sugar, put them in a pretty box, tie a colourful ribbon around them and give them to friends and family as gifts. You'll be very popular!

Ricciarelli

2 egg whites

a pinch of sea salt

225 g/1 cup caster/granulated sugar

grated zest of 1 lemon

½ teaspoon vanilla extract

1 teaspoon almond extract

300 g/2 cups ground almonds

4 tablespoons flaked/slivered almonds

icing/confectioners' sugar, for dusting

2 baking sheets, lined with baking parchment

Makes about 20 biscuits

Preheat the oven to 150°C (300°F) Gas 2.

Put the egg whites in a large, clean mixing bowl with the salt and use an electric whisk to beat them to stiff peaks.

Gradually add the sugar, whisking constantly until completely incorporated. Add the lemon zest, vanilla extract and almond extract and mix again. Fold in the ground almonds using a large metal spoon or spatula.

Wet your hands under the tap, then pull off a bit of the dough, about the size of a walnut, and roll it into a ball. Put it on one of the baking sheet and flatten slightly. Keep doing this until you have used all the dough.

Sprinkle flaked/slivered almonds over each ricciarelli.

Put the baking sheets on the middle shelf of the preheated oven. Bake for about 25 minutes, or until pale gold. Leave the ricciarelli to cool, then dust with icing/confectioners' sugar.

Shortbread

175 g/1⅓ cups plain/all-purpose flour

25 g/3 tablespoons rice flour, fine semolina or cornflour/cornstarch

75 g/⅓ cup caster/granulated sugar, plus extra for sprinkling

a pinch of salt

175 g/1½ sticks unsalted butter, chilled and diced

a baking sheet, lined with baking parchment

Makes 8 wedges

This is a popular Christmas biscuit that can either be made the traditional way – in a circle – and cut into wedges, or in a rectangle and then cut into fingers. You could always flavour the basic shortbread dough with lemon zest or even some stem ginger, if you like.

Sift the flour, rice flour, sugar and salt into a large mixing bowl. Add the chilled butter and rub in with your fingertips until you get a ball of dough.

Sprinkle a little flour on a clean work surface. Tip the dough out of the bowl and onto the work surface. Press or roll the dough into a circle about 20 cm/8 inches across. Alternatively, you can flatten the dough into a rough rectangle.

Carefully lift the shortbread dough onto the prepared baking sheet. Working your way around the edge of the circle, press the dough between your thumb and forefinger to create a crinkled border.

Using a knife, mark 8 wedges into the shortbread, but don't cut all the way through. Chill the shortbread dough in the fridge for 30 minutes.

Preheat the oven to 150°C (300°F) Gas 2.

Prick the shortbread all over with a fork and sprinkle with more sugar. Put the baking sheet on the middle shelf of the preheated oven. Bake for about 45–50 minutes until light golden.

Leave the shortbread to cool a little before cutting into wedges, following the marks you made before baking.

Hazelnut tea cookies

75 g/5 tablespoons butter, at room temperature

25 g/3 tablespoons icing/confectioners' sugar, sifted, plus extra for rolling

¼ teaspoon vanilla extract

40 g/⅓ cup toasted hazelnuts, finely chopped

100 g/⅔ cup plain/all-purpose flour

a baking sheet, lined with baking parchment

Makes 12 cookies

Frequently referred to as Russian teacakes, these plump, round, sugared cookies look wonderful piled up on a dainty plate, like little snowballs. These are made with hazelnuts, but popular variations are made with almonds and walnuts.

Preheat the oven to 180°C (350°F) Gas 4. Put the butter and icing/confectioners' sugar in a bowl and beat until smooth. Add the vanilla extract and hazelnuts and mix to combine. Add the flour and bring the mixture together to make a stiff dough.

With cool hands, roll the dough into 12 balls – each about 3 cm/1 inch in diameter – and arrange them on the prepared baking sheet. Bake for about 12 minutes, until a pale golden colour.

Spoon about 4 generous tablespoons/¼ cup of icing/confectioners' sugar into a wide, shallow bowl. While the cookies are still hot from the oven, roll them in the sugar to coat, then transfer to a wire rack to cool. When completely cool, roll in sugar a second time to coat. (Add more sugar to the bowl if necessary.)

Double chocolate chip cookies

These large, flat cookies are perfect for sandwiching together with ice cream. To make smaller ones for eating with milk, use smaller spoonfuls and don't spread the mixture out. Although real chopped chocolate tastes better, it won't hold its shape as nicely as ready-made chocolate chips. For real chocoholics, use cacao nibs instead.

75 g/5 tablespoons unsalted butter, at room temperature

75 g/5 tablespoons golden caster/granulated sugar

75 g/5 tablespoons light brown soft sugar, sifted

1 large egg, beaten

½ teaspoon vanilla or chocolate extract

150 g/1 cup plus 2 tablespoons self-raising flour

25 g/3 tablespoons unsweetened cocoa powder

¼ teaspoon salt

100 g/⅔ cup dark/bittersweet and white (or milk) chocolate chips (or roughly chopped chocolate)

a heavy, non-stick baking sheet

Makes 12 large cookies

Preheat the oven to 180°C (350°F) Gas 4.

Using an electric whisk, cream the butter and sugars together until pale and fluffy. Beat in the egg and vanilla extract.

Sift the flour with the cocoa and salt in a small bowl. Fold into the egg mixture with the chocolate chips.

Place 4 heaped tablespoonfuls of the mixture on the prepared baking sheet, spacing them well apart. Press down and spread out to about 5 mm/⅛ inch thick with the back of a wet spoon or with dampened fingers (you may like to scatter some more chocolate chips over the top). Bake in the preheated oven for 10–12 minutes. Leave to cool on the baking sheet for 1 minute, then transfer to a wire rack. When cool, store in an airtight container. Repeat with the remaining mixture.

Macarons have made a comeback in recent years and are now sold in all sorts of pretty colours. This is a simple way of making them and you can buy very good, luxury lemon or orange curd, which is ideal for filling them.

St. clement's macarons

100 g/⅔ cup ground almonds

150 g/¾ cup caster/
granulated sugar

2 teaspoons plain/
all-purpose flour

2 large egg whites

grated zest of 1 lemon

grated zest of ½ orange

Filling

3 tablespoons cream cheese

3 tablespoons thick lemon
or orange curd

grated zest of ½ orange

*2 baking sheets, lined with
baking parchment*

Makes 12 macarons

Preheat the oven to 180°C (350°F) Gas 4.

Tip all the ingredients (other than those for the filling) into an electric mixer. Alternatively, put them in a large mixing bowl and use an electric whisk. Beat together until well combined.

Put 24 teaspoonfuls of the mixture onto the prepared baking sheets, leaving room for them to spread slightly. Bake in the preheated oven for 15–17 minutes, or until set and tinged with gold at the edges. Leave to cool for a few minutes, then transfer to wire racks.

To make the filling, whisk the cream cheese and curd together until smooth. Stir in the orange zest and refrigerate until needed. Sandwich the macarons together with the filling.

Sugared refrigerator cookies

225 g/15 tablespoons unsalted butter, softened

125 g/⅔ cup caster/granulated sugar

1 egg, beaten

1 teaspoon vanilla extract

300 g/2⅓ cups plain/all-purpose flour, plus extra for dusting

a pinch of salt

4 tablespoons granulated sugar

yellow, red, green and/or purple food colouring pastes to match your colour scheme

1 tablespoon milk

Flavourings

2 tablespoons finely chopped mixed peel or 125 g/4 oz. chopped glacé cherries or 125 g/4 oz. chopped pistachios or 2 tablespoons dried lavender flowers, to match your colour scheme

2 baking sheets, lined with baking parchment

Makes about 20 cookies

This simple shortbread can be adapted into a rainbow of flavours and colours. Match the colour of the sugar to the flavour of the cookies: yellow for lemon, green for pistachio and purple for lavender. Decide on one flavour and corresponding colour scheme before you start.

Cream together the butter and caster/granulated sugar until light and creamy in the bowl of a freestanding mixer (or use an electric whisk and mixing bowl). Add the egg and vanilla and mix well. Sift the flour and salt into the mixture, along with the flavouring you have chosen, and mix again until smooth and the flour is incorporated.

Tip the dough onto a very lightly floured work surface and divide into 2. Roll each piece of dough into a sausage shape roughly 5 cm/2 inches in diameter, wrap tightly in parchment paper and refrigerate until solid – at least 2 hours.

Preheat the oven to 150°C (300°F) Gas 3.

Tip the granulated sugar into a plastic food bag. Using the tip of a wooden skewer, gradually add the colour of food colouring paste you have chosen to match the flavour of the cookie, mixing well until the desired shade is reached. Tip the coloured sugar onto a baking sheet. Remove the cookie dough logs from the fridge and brush them with the milk. Roll in the coloured sugar to coat evenly.

Using a sharp knife, cut the logs into 5-mm/¼-inch slices and arrange on the prepared baking sheet. Bake on the middle shelf of the preheated oven for about 15 minutes, or until pale golden. Leave to cool on the sheets for 5 minutes before transferring to a wire rack to cool completely.

125 g/1 stick unsalted butter

200 g/1 cup dark brown soft sugar

1 large egg

1 teaspoon vanilla extract

280 g/2 cups plus 2 tablespoons self-raising flour

40 g/⅓ cup cocoa powder

1 teaspoon baking powder

½ teaspoon salt

250 ml/1 cup buttermilk

Rose and violet fillings

250 ml/1 cup double/heavy cream

250 g/1 cup mascarpone

2 tablespoons icing/confectioners' sugar

1 tablespoon rose syrup

1 tablespoon violet syrup

pink and purple food colourings

To decorate

150 g/5½ oz. dark chocolate

crystallized rose and violet petals

two baking sheets, lined with baking parchment

a piping bag fitted with a large round nozzle/tip (optional)

two piping bags, each fitted with a medium round nozzle/tip

24 foil petit four cases

Makes 24 pies

Rose and violet cream pies

These gorgeous whoopie pies take their inspiration from old-fashioned rose and violet cream chocolates with their floral fondant fillings, rich dark chocolate shells and crystallized rose and violet petal decorations.

Preheat the oven to 180°C (350°F) Gas 4.

To make the pies, cream together the butter and brown sugar in a mixing bowl for 2–3 minutes using an electric hand-held mixer, until light and creamy. Add the egg and vanilla extract and mix again. Sift the flour, cocoa and baking powder into the bowl and add the salt and buttermilk. Whisk again until everything is incorporated. Add 100 ml/⅓ cup hot (not boiling) water and whisk into the mixture.

Spoon the mixture into the piping bag with the large nozzle and pipe 48 rounds onto the prepared sheets (about 3-cm/1-inch diameter) leaving a gap between each pie as they will spread during baking. (Alternatively, use 2 teaspoons to form small rounds on the sheets.) Leave to stand for 10 minutes then bake each sheet in the preheated oven for 10–12 minutes. Remove the pies from the oven, let cool slightly then transfer to a wire rack to cool.

To make the fillings, whip the cream to stiff peaks. In a separate bowl, beat the mascarpone until softened then fold it into the whipped cream along with the icing/confectioners' sugar. Transfer half of the mixture to a separate bowl; add the rose syrup and a few drops of pink food colouring to 1 bowl and the violet syrup and a drop of purple food colouring to the other. Mix both creams well with an electric hand-held mixer.

Spoon the fillings into the 2 remaining piping bags and pipe circles of each flavour onto 12 pie halves, so that you have 24 pie halves covered with cream. Top with the remaining pie halves. To decorate, melt the chocolate. Spoon a little melted chocolate on each pie, top with a crystallized rose or violet petal, as appropriate to the filling, and allow to set. Put them in petit four cases.

Ginger and chilli caramel cookies

50 g/3 tablespoons unsalted butter, at room temperature

100 g/½ cup golden caster/granulated sugar

1 egg

50 g/½ cup finely chopped crystallized ginger

130 g/1 cup plain/all-purpose flour

1½ teaspoons baking powder

2 teaspoons ground ginger

Chilli caramel

100 g/½ cup golden caster/granulated sugar

a pinch of ground cayenne pepper or hot chilli powder (or more if you like the heat!)

1–2 baking sheets, lined with baking parchment

Makes about 15 cookies

These addictive cookies are drizzled with hot caramel, so you can explore your artistic side when it comes to decorating them! With a generous dose of crystallized ginger and bit of chilli heat, they are not for the faint-hearted.

Preheat the oven to 160°C (325°F) Gas 3.

Cream the butter and sugar in a mixing bowl until light and fluffy. Add the egg and mix well, then stir in the crystallized ginger. Mix the flour, baking powder and ground ginger in a separate bowl, then gently fold into the wet ingredients.

Take a generous teaspoon of the dough and place on one of the prepared baking sheets. Flatten it slightly, then repeat this process with the remaining dough, spacing the dough balls well apart as they will spread when baking.

Bake in the preheated oven for about 25 minutes, or until the cookies are golden. Remove from the oven and leave to cool.

To make the chilli caramel, put the sugar in a heavy-based saucepan over medium heat. The sugar can burn quite easily (which can render the caramel bitter), so stir it often and keep a close eye on it. After a few minutes, the sugar should have completely melted. Remove from the heat and stir in the pepper or chilli powder. Be very careful when handling caramel as it can easily burn you. Use it immediately before it starts to harden.

Using a spoon, drizzle the caramel over the biscuits. The caramel sets extremely quickly. When it has set, remove the biscuits from the sheet.

Walnut and cinnamon macarons

60 g/generous ½ cup
ground almonds

60 g/½ cup walnut pieces

25 g/1 generous tablespoon
dark brown soft sugar

2 teaspoons ground cinnamon

150 g/1 cup powdered fondant
icing/confectioners' sugar

3 egg whites (about 90 g/3¼ oz.)

75 g/⅓ cup caster/superfine
sugar

a few drops of orange food
colouring

Filling

100 g/1 cup walnut pieces

50 g/3½ tablespoons butter

200 g/1½ cups icing/
confectioners' sugar

2 tablespoons double/
heavy cream

*2 piping bags, both fitted with
large round nozzles/tips*

a baking sheet, lined

Makes 12 macarons

*These walnut and cinnamon macarons are an earthy twist
on a traditional, and very chic, French classic.*

Put the ground almonds, walnuts, brown sugar, cinnamon and fondant
icing/confectioners' sugar in a food processor and blitz to a very fine
powder. Sift into a mixing bowl and return any pieces that do not pass
through the sieve/strainer to the blender, blitz, then sift again.

Whisk the egg whites to stiff peaks, adding the caster/superfine sugar
a spoonful at a time, until the meringue is smooth and glossy. Use a
spatula to fold in the walnut mixture a third at a time, along with a few
drops of food colouring. It needs to be folded until it is soft enough to
just not hold a peak. Drop a little onto a plate and if it folds to a smooth
surface it is ready. If it holds a peak then you need to fold it a few
further times. If you fold it too much it will be too runny and the
macarons will not retain their shape.

Spoon the mixture into one of the piping bags. Pipe 6-cm/2½- in rounds
onto the baking sheet a small distance apart. Leave to set on the baking
sheets for 1 hour so that the surface of the macarons forms a skin.

Preheat the oven to 170°C (325°F) Gas 3. Bake in the preheated oven
for 15–20 minutes, until firm. Leave to cool on the baking sheets.

Meanwhile make the filling. Blitz the walnuts in a food processor until
very finely chopped. Add the butter and blend again. Transfer to a
mixing bowl with the icing/confectioners' sugar and cream and whisk
together until light. Spoon the filling into the second piping bag and
pipe a swirl onto half of the cooled macarons. Top each with a second
macaron and serve.

These macarons will keep for up to 3 days if stored in an airtight
container.

Florentines

These nutty, fruity nibbles dipped in chocolate are perfect after-dinner Christmas treats served with coffee or tea. They can even be gift-wrapped and used as stocking fillers. But you don't have to wait until Christmas to eat them.

60 g/4 tablespoons unsalted butter

60 g/⅓ cup golden caster/granulated sugar

60 g/¼ cup runny honey

60 g/½ cup plain/all-purpose flour

35 g/¼ cup mixed peel

35 g/¼ cup dried cranberries

65 g/½ cup sultanas/golden raisins

45 g/⅓ cup flaked/slivered almonds, plus extra to sprinkle

35 g/⅓ cup shelled walnuts, chopped

35 g/⅓ cup shelled pecan nuts, chopped

80 g/2½ oz. dark/bittersweet chocolate, chopped

1–2 baking sheets, greased

Makes 20 florentines

Preheat the oven to 150°C (300°F) Gas 2.

Put the butter, sugar and honey in a saucepan over medium heat and gently bring to the boil. Do not let the ingredients burn. When it reaches boiling point, stir until the sugar has dissolved completely, then remove from the heat.

Stir in the flour, mixed peel, cranberries, sultanas/golden raisins, almonds, walnuts and pecan nuts. Mix until well combined. Leave to cool for a while before handling.

Take a generous teaspoon of the mixture, roughly roll into a ball and place on one of the prepared baking sheets. Flatten it gently, then repeat this process with the remaining mixture, spacing the discs apart as they may spread when they are baking. Sprinkle a few flaked almonds over each florentine.

Bake in the preheated oven for 15 minutes. Remove from the oven and leave to cool.

In the meantime, put the chocolate in a heatproof bowl over a saucepan of barely simmering water. Do not let the base of the bowl touch the water. Stir until melted. Dip one side of each florentine in the bowl of melted chocolate and leave to set, chocolate side up, on a cooling rack. Store in an airtight container for up to 2 weeks.

80 g/3 oz. dark/bittersweet chocolate

125 g/1 stick unsalted butter or vegetable shortening, softened

200 g/1 cup dark brown soft sugar

1 large egg

300 g/2¼ cups plus 2 tablespoons self-raising flour

20 g/2½ tablespoons cocoa powder

1 teaspoon baking powder

½ teaspoon salt

250 ml/1 cup plain yogurt

Cherry cream filling

200 g/1 cup fresh cherries, pitted

2 tablespoons caster/granulated sugar

2 tablespoons kirsch (optional)

350 ml/1⅓ cups double/heavy cream, whipped

Chocolate glaze

45 g/3 tablespoons unsalted butter

90 ml/⅓ cup golden/corn syrup

100 g/3⅓ oz. dark/semisweet chocolate, broken into pieces

12 fresh cherries with stalks on, to decorate

two 12-hole whoopie pie tins/pans, greased

Makes 12 pies

Chocolate and cherry pies

These indulgent whoopie pies are a heady combination of cherries, chocolate and kirsch. For an alcohol-free version omit the kirsch.

Preheat the oven to 180°C (350°F) Gas 4.

To make the pies, first melt the dark/semisweet chocolate. Cream together the butter and brown sugar in a mixing bowl for 2–3 minutes using an electric hand-held mixer, until light and creamy. Add the egg and mix again. Sift the flour, cocoa and baking powder into the bowl and add the salt, melted chocolate and yogurt. Whisk again until everything is incorporated. Add 100 ml/⅓ cup hot (not boiling) water and whisk into the mixture.

Put a large spoonful of mixture into each hole in the prepared tins/pans. Leave to stand for 10 minutes then bake each tin/pan for 10–12 minutes in the preheated oven. Remove the pies from the oven, let cool slightly then turn out onto a wire rack.

To make the cherry cream filling, put the cherries in a saucepan with the caster/granulated sugar and 100 ml/⅓ cup cold water. Simmer over low heat until soft, then remove from the heat. Stir in the kirsch (if using) and set aside to cool. When cooled, fold the cherry compote into the whipped cream, cover and chill in the fridge until needed.

To make the chocolate glaze, heat the butter with the syrup, chocolate and 40 ml/2½ tablespoons cold water in a saucepan, until the chocolate and butter have melted and you have a shiny syrup. Spoon the glaze over 12 of the pie halves. Top each one with a fresh cherry and allow to set for a few minutes.

Spoon some cherry cream filling onto the unglazed pie halves and spread with a round-bladed-knife. Top each one with a glazed and cherry-topped pie half and your whoopie pies are ready to enjoy.

White chocolate and fresh raspberry cookies

125 g/1 stick unsalted butter, at room temperature

75 g/⅓ cup golden caster/granulated sugar

150 g/1 cup plus 3 tablespoons self-raising flour

1 tablespoon whole milk

1 teaspoon vanilla extract

100 g/3½ oz. white chocolate, chopped

100 g/1 scant cup fresh or frozen raspberries (if using frozen, allow them to soften for a few minutes before using)

3 baking sheets, lined with baking parchment

Makes 12 cookies

The flavours of fresh raspberries and white chocolate work brilliantly well together. This recipe is quick and easy to make and so tasty that you will be wanting to bake these cookies regularly!

Preheat the oven to 180°C (350°F) Gas 4.

Cream the butter and sugar together in a bowl until light and fluffy. Add the flour and milk and mix into a dough.

Stir in the vanilla extract and chocolate. Mash the raspberries gently with a fork and stir them into the mixture. (This helps distribute the raspberries and also tinges the dough a lovely pink colour.)

Use your hands to divide the dough into 12 balls. Arrange 4 balls on each baking sheet, leaving plenty of space between them as they will spread as they bake. Shape each cookie gently with your fingers to make chunky rounds about 5 cm/2 inches in diameter (they will spread to about 9 cm/3½ inches in diameter). Bake in the preheated oven for about 15 minutes, until golden brown.

Allow the cookies to cool and firm up on the baking sheets for a few minutes before transferring them to a wire rack.

Eat as soon as the cookies are cool enough to handle as they are definitely best eaten freshly baked and still warm.

As these cookies contain fresh fruit, they will be at their best for only 2–3 days.

Pound and Loaf Cakes

Lemon loaf with white chocolate frosting

The rich, citrussy base and creamy white chocolate frosting are fabulously matched in this perfect teatime cake.

65 g/4 tablespoons unsalted butter, at room temperature

135 g/⅔ cup golden caster/granulated sugar

2 eggs

135 g/1 cup plain/all-purpose flour

1½ teaspoons baking powder

finely grated zest and freshly squeezed juice of 2 lemons

White chocolate icing

150 g/5 oz. white chocolate, chopped, plus extra, grated, to decorate

75 ml/⅓ cup double/heavy cream

a 17 x 9-cm/6 x 4½-inch loaf tin/pan, lined with baking parchment

Serves 6

Preheat the oven to 170°C (325°F) Gas 3.

Put the butter and sugar in a mixing bowl and mix well with an electric whisk. Add the eggs and whisk for a couple of minutes until pale and fluffy. Gently fold in the flour and baking powder. Finally, stir in the lemon zest and juice until well mixed.

Pour the mixture into the prepared loaf tin/pan and bake in the preheated oven for 25 minutes. When it's ready, the cake will be a rich golden colour and springy to the touch. Remove it from the oven and turn out onto a wire rack to cool before frosting.

In the meantime, make the white chocolate frosting. Put the chocolate in a mixing bowl. Put the cream in a saucepan and gently bring to the boil over low heat, stirring frequently. Pour into the mixing bowl and whisk until you get a smooth cream. Leave to cool for a couple of minutes, then refrigerate for 15 minutes to stiffen.

Spread the frosting on top of the cake and sprinkle some grated chocolate over it.

Mocha swirl loaf with espresso icing

1 slightly rounded tablespoon espresso instant coffee powder

200 g/¾ cup fromage frais

75 g/½ cup polenta/cornmeal

125 g/1 stick butter, softened

225 g/1 cup caster/granulated sugar

3 large eggs

200 g/1⅔ cups self-raising flour

½ teaspoon bicarbonate of soda/baking soda

1 teaspoon vanilla extract

2 teaspoons cocoa powder

Espresso icing

100 g/⅔ cup icing/confectioners' sugar

1 slightly rounded teaspoon espresso instant coffee powder

a 19 x 9-cm/8½ x 4½-inch loaf tin/pan, lightly buttered and base-lined with baking parchment

Serves 8–10

The fromage frais in this loaf keeps the fat content down and the polenta gives it a lovely crunchy crust.

Preheat the oven to 180°C (350°F) Gas 4.

Put the espresso powder in a cup with one tablespoon boiling water and stir to dissolve, then leave to cool.

Next, take a scant tablespoon from the fromage frais and set it aside for the icing. Put the remaining fromage frais with the polenta/cornmeal, butter, sugar, eggs, flour and bicarbonate of soda/baking soda in an electric mixer (or use a large mixing bowl and an electric whisk) and beat until combined. Transfer half the mixture to another bowl. Stir the vanilla extract into the first bowl. Stir the dissolved coffee and the cocoa into the second bowl.

Spoon the 2 mixtures into the prepared loaf tin/pan in 3 layers, alternating spoonfuls of each mixture in each layer to resemble a chequerboard. Finally, using a skewer, gently swirl the layers together a few times until you have a definite swirl pattern on top of the loaf.

Bake in the preheated oven for 55 minutes, or until risen and the loaf is a lovely golden colour on top. Leave to cool in the tin/pan.

To make the espresso icing, sift the icing/confectioners' sugar into a bowl and mix in the espresso powder along with the reserved tablespoon of fromage frais. Add enough cold water to make the icing a spreadable consistency – about 2 teaspoonfuls – but add it gradually, stirring, as you might not need it all.

Run a knife around the edges of the cold loaf in the tin/pan to release it. Turn it out, remove the base paper and spread the icing on top of the loaf. Leave to set before slicing.

Banana and passion-fruit loaf

225 g/1¾ cups self-raising flour

½ teaspoon bicarbonate of soda/baking soda

100 g/6½ tablespoons butter, softened and cubed

175 g/¾ cup granulated sugar

2 large eggs, lightly beaten

3 passion fruit

3 very ripe bananas

To decorate

100 g/¾ cup icing/confectioners' sugar

1 passion fruit

dried banana slices, to decorate

a 19 x 9-cm/8½ x 4½-inch loaf tin/pan, buttered and base-lined with baking parchment

Serves 8–10

For the best flavour, make sure your bananas are really ripe for this, even if they are at the stage when they have turned black in the fruit bowl and no one wants to eat them; they will be perfect to use in this loaf.

Preheat the oven to 180°C (350°F) Gas 4.

Sift the flour and bicarbonate of soda/baking soda into a bowl. Put the butter and sugar in an electric mixer (or use a large mixing bowl and an electric whisk) and beat until pale and fluffy. Add the beaten eggs and sifted flour mixture alternately to the bowl.

Halve the passion fruit and scoop out the pulp into a sieve/strainer over a bowl. Using a teaspoon, press and stir the pulp to extract the juice. Discard the leftover seeds. Peel and mash the bananas. Add the passion fruit pulp and mashed banana to the cake mixture and mix again.

Tip the mixture into the prepared loaf tin/pan and spread it evenly with a spatula. Bake in the preheated oven for 55 minutes, or until golden and risen. Leave to cool in the tin/pan.

To decorate, sift the icing/confectioners' sugar into a small bowl. Halve the passion fruit and scoop out the pulp into the bowl – no need to sieve/strain the pulp this time. Mix together with a teaspoon. If the glaze seems a little thick, add a drop or two of cold water – the consistency of the glaze will depend on the size of the passion fruit and how ripe it is. You want the glaze to be a thick, spreadable consistency.

Tip the cold loaf out of the tin/pan and peel off the base paper. Spoon the glaze over the top of the loaf and decorate with dried banana slices. Leave to set for about 30 minutes before slicing.

Pain d'épices

225 g/1¾ cups plain/all-purpose flour

2 teaspoons baking powder

1 teaspoon ground cinnamon

3 teaspoons ground ginger

¼ teaspoon ground allspice

¼ teaspoon ground cloves

¼ teaspoon salt

150 g/10 tablespoons unsalted butter, softened

75 g/⅓ cup light brown soft sugar

125 ml/½ cup clear honey

2 eggs, lightly beaten

3–4 tablespoons milk

a 900 g/2-lb. loaf tin/pan, greased and lined with baking parchment

Serves 8–10

This is a delicious French gingerbread cake. Make it a couple of days before you want to eat it so that the flavours of all the spices have time to mellow with the honey. Serve it in slices on its own or with a lick of butter.

Preheat the oven to 180°C (350°F) Gas 4.

Sift the flour, baking powder, cinnamon, ginger, allspice, cloves and salt together into a mixing bowl and set aside.

Put the butter and sugar in the bowl of an electric mixer (or use a large mixing bowl and an electric whisk) and cream them until pale and light.

Add the honey and mix again. Gradually add the beaten eggs, mixing well between each addition and scraping down the bowl with a rubber spatula from time to time.

Add the sifted dry ingredients and the milk and mix again until smooth. Spoon into the prepared loaf tin/pan and spread evenly with a knife.

Bake in the preheated oven for about 1 hour, or until well risen and a skewer inserted into the middle of the cake comes out clean. You may need to cover the cake loosely with a sheet of foil if it is browning too quickly.

Leave it to cool in the tin/pan for 5 minutes before tipping out onto a wire rack to cool completely.

Fresh orange cake

This an easy to make all-in-one loaf cake flavoured with fresh orange. Look out for an unwaxed or organic orange, as half of it will be whizzed up in a processor, and the other half used for the topping.

1 orange

175 g/1½ sticks unsalted butter, very soft

250 g/1¼ cups caster/ granulated sugar

3 large free-range eggs, at room temperature

250 g/2 cups self-raising flour, sifted

1 teaspoon bicarbonate of soda/baking soda

100 ml/scant ½ cup milk

3 tablespoons plain yogurt (not fat-free)

3 tablespoons granulated sugar, for the topping

a 900 g/2 lb. loaf tin, greased and lined with baking parchment

Serves 8–10

Preheat the oven to 180°C (350°F) Gas 4.

Cut the orange in half, reserving one half for the topping. Remove the pips from the other half then cut it into 8 pieces. Put the pieces (skin still on) in a food processor and blitz until the orange is chopped into very small pieces. Transfer the orange mixture to a large mixing bowl.

Add the butter and sugar to the mixing bowl and break in the eggs. Sift the flour and bicarbonate of soda/baking soda into the bowl. Add the milk and yogurt then beat with a wooden spoon or electric mixer (on low speed) for 1 minute until well mixed and there are no streaks of flour visible.

Spoon the mixture into the prepared tin/pan and bake in the preheated oven for about 50 minutes, until a good golden brown and a skewer inserted into the middle of the cake comes out clean.

Meanwhile, make the topping. Squeeze the juice from the reserved orange half, add to a small bowl with the sugar and stir to make a thick, syrupy glaze.

Remove the loaf from the oven and stand the tin/pan on a wire rack. Prick the top of the loaf all over with a skewer to make lots of small holes. Spoon the orange syrup all over the top so it trickles into the holes. Leave until completely cold before removing the cake from the tin/pan, peeling off the lining paper and slicing.

Blueberry lemon pound cake

250 g/2¼ sticks unsalted butter, at room temperature

250 g/1¼ cups caster/granulated sugar

grated zest of 1 large lemon

4 large eggs, at room temperature

a pinch of salt

250 g/1¾ cups self-raising flour

75 g/½ cup dried blueberries

icing/confectioners' sugar, for dusting

a 27 x 18-cm/11½ x 8½-inch daisy, non-stick cake tin/pan, or roasting tin/pan, greased

Serves 8–10

This traditional cake, made with equal weights of butter, sugar, eggs and flour, needs plenty of beating to add air and lightness. Here the hard work is done with an electric mixer, and the dried berries add a burst of flavour.

Put the butter in an electric mixer and beat at low speed until creamy. Increase the speed and gradually beat in the sugar, followed by the lemon zest.

Put the eggs and salt in a jug/pitcher, beat lightly, then add to the creamed mixture, 1 tablespoon or so at a time, beating well after each addition. Add 1 tablespoon flour with the 2 last portions of egg to prevent the mixture from separating.

Sift the rest of the flour onto the mixture and gently fold in with a large metal spoon. When you no longer see streaks of flour, mix in the blueberries.

Transfer to the prepared tin/pan and spread evenly. Bake in a preheated oven at 180°C (350°F) Gas 4 for about 40 minutes or until a skewer inserted in the centre comes out clean. Let cool in the tin/pan for 10 minutes, then carefully turn out onto a wire rack to cool completely. Dust with icing/confectioners' sugar before serving.

Store in an airtight container and eat within 5 days.

Russian poppy seed cake

115 g/¾ cup poppy seeds

160 ml/⅔ cup milk

125 g/1 stick butter, at room temperature

250 g/1⅓ cups caster/granulated sugar

1 teaspoon vanilla extract

2 eggs, separated

200 g/1⅓ cups plain/all-purpose flour

2 teaspoons baking powder

¼ teaspoon sea salt

icing/confectioners' sugar, for dusting

a 900-g/2-lb loaf tin/pan, greased

Serves 8–12

You will find versions of this classic cake all over Russia, the Ukraine and Eastern Europe. It is delicious eaten with the strong, dark tea favoured by Russians. The poppy seeds give it a subtle yet distinctive flavour and striking dark appearance when you cut into it.

Put the poppy seeds in a food processor or blender and process for about 1 minute, until finely chopped and almost damp-looking in appearance. Tip the seeds into a saucepan, pour in the milk and bring to the boil, stirring once or twice. Remove from the heat and leave to sit for about 1 hour.

Preheat the oven to 180°C (350°F) Gas 4.

Put the butter and sugar in a bowl and beat until smooth and creamy. Beat in the vanilla extract and egg yolks. Add the poppy seed and milk mixture and mix well until thoroughly combined.

Combine the flour, baking powder and salt. Sift it into the poppy seed mixture and fold in. Put the egg whites in a separate, grease-free bowl and whisk until stiff, then fold into the cake mixture a few tablespoonfuls at a time. Tip the mixture into the prepared loaf tin/pan and level the surface. Bake for about 1 hour, or until a skewer inserted in the centre of the cake comes out clean. Remove from the oven, then lift the cake out of the tin/pan and leave to cool on a wire rack. Dust liberally with icing/confectioners' sugar to serve.

finely grated zest of 1 lemon

250 g/8 oz. marzipan

1 egg, beaten

100 g/7 tablespoons unsalted butter, melted

150 g/1 cup icing/confectioners' sugar

Rum-soaked fruits

250 g/1½ cups sultanas/golden raisins

170 g/1½ cups mixed peel

80 ml/⅓ cup dark or golden rum

Stollen dough

1 tablespoon dried quick yeast

70 g/⅓ cup golden caster/granulated sugar

140 ml/½ cup plus 1 tablespoon whole milk, warmed

1 large egg yolk

175 g/1½ sticks unsalted butter, at room temperature

500 g/3¾ cups strong/bread flour

a baking sheet, lined with baking parchment

Makes 2 stollen

Stollen

This is a labour-intensive but rewarding traditional Christmas sweet filled with rum-soaked fruits and plenty of marzipan.

Prepare the rum-soaked fruits at least 24 hours in advance. Put the sultanas/golden raisins, mixed peel and rum in a bowl. Mix, cover and leave to rest for at least 24 hours.

When you are ready to make the stollen dough, stir the yeast and sugar into the warm milk and set aside for 5 minutes.

Put the egg yolk, butter and flour in a mixing bowl and add the yeast mixture. Mix until you get a smooth dough, then transfer to a lightly floured surface and knead for 5 minutes. The dough should be soft but not sticky. If it is sticky, add a little flour and knead again. Return the dough to the mixing bowl, dust in flour, cover and leave to rise for 1 hour in a warm place. The dough should increase significantly in size.

Stir the lemon zest into the rum-soaked fruits, then uncover your mixing bowl and pour in the soaked fruits. Knead the dough again to incorporate and evenly distribute the fruits. Divide the dough in two, cover, and leave to rise for another 40 minutes in a warm place.

Take one ball of dough and roll it out with a rolling pin into a rough square about 5 mm/¼ inch thick. Take half the marzipan and roll it into a tube slightly shorter than the square of dough. Place it along one side of the dough and start to roll the dough up from that side. Keep the sides tucked in as you roll. Repeat with the other ball of dough and remaining marzipan. Brush the beaten egg over the stollen. Cover and leave to rise for another 30 minutes in a warm place.

Preheat the oven to 200°C (400°F) Gas 6. Put the logs on the prepared baking sheet and bake for 10 minutes, then reduce the heat to 190°C (375°F) Gas 5 and bake for another 20 minutes. Remove from the oven and brush the stollen with melted butter. Dust with icing/confectioners' sugar and leave to cool.

300 g/2⅓ cups plain/all-purpose flour

50 g/6 tablespoons unsweetened cocoa powder

3 teaspoons baking powder

½ teaspoon bicarbonate of soda/baking soda

½ teaspoon salt

350 ml/1⅓ cups milk

100 g/⅔ cup amarena cherries, plus 100 ml/6 tablespoons of their syrup

75 g/⅓ cup light brown soft sugar

50 g/3 tablespoons unsalted butter, softened

100 g/3½ oz. dark/bittersweet chocolate, broken into pieces

150 g/1 cup macadamia nuts, roughly chopped, plus extra to scatter

eight mini or two 450-g/1-lb. loaf tins/pans

Makes 8 mini teabreads or 2 large teabreads

There's something about the combination of dark chocolate and bitter cherries that is beguiling. These moist little teabreads are studded with those succulent cherries in syrup often found spooned over ice cream in Italian ice cream parlours. Creamy macadamia nuts add an extra layer of luxury to these already decadent teabreads.

Chocolate, cherry and macadamia teabreads

Preheat the oven to 150°C (300°F) Gas 2. Grease the loaf tins/pans, base-line with non-stick baking parchment and dust with flour.

Sift the flour, cocoa, baking powder, bicarbonate of soda/baking soda and salt together in a large bowl.

Heat the milk, amarena cherry syrup, sugar, butter and chocolate together in a medium pan until melted and smooth. Stir this into the flour mixture as quickly and deftly as possible until just combined – as if you were making muffins. Stir in the cherries and macadamia nuts, then spoon into the tins/pans and smooth the surface. Scatter with extra macadamia nuts.

Bake for about 30 minutes for the smaller tins and 1 hour for the larger tins/pans, or until firm. A metal skewer inserted into the centre should come out clean. Remove from the oven and leave to cool in the tins/pans for 10 minutes. Turn out onto a wire rack and leave to cool completely. Store in an airtight container for 1 day to mature before serving.

230 g/2 sticks unsalted butter, at room temperature

230 g/1 cup plus 2 tablespoons caster/granulated sugar

4 large eggs, at room temperature

3 tablespoons milk, brandy or bourbon

½ teaspoon vanilla extract

75 g/1 cup mixed raisins and sultanas/golden raisins

100 g/1 cup pecan nuts, coarsely chopped

230 g/1¾ cups self-raising flour

a pinch of salt

¼ teaspoon ground mace

¼ teaspoon freshly grated nutmeg

icing/confectioners' sugar, for dusting

a 23-cm/9-inch Bundt tin/pan, well greased,

Makes one Bundt cake or loaf cake

Festive fruit and nut pound cake

This pound cake may contain extra Christmas cheer, depending whether or not you decide to replace the milk with brandy, or bourbon. Either way, it's delicious!

Put the butter and sugar in a bowl and, using an electric mixer, beat well until light and fluffy. Break the eggs into a jug/pitcher, add the milk (or brandy or bourbon) and vanilla extract and mix with a fork. Gradually beat into the butter mixture, about 1 tablespoon at a time, beating well after each addition.

Put the fruit and pecans in a bowl, add 1 tablespoon of the flour and toss gently.

Sift the remaining flour, salt, mace and nutmeg onto the creamed mixture and gently fold in with a large metal spoon. Add the fruit and pecans to the cake mixture and stir gently. Transfer to the prepared tin/pan and spread evenly.

Bake in a preheated oven at 180°C (350°F) Gas 4 for 45–50 minutes, or until a skewer inserted in the thickest part of the cake comes out clean. Let cool in the tin/pan, then turn out onto a wire rack to cool completely. Serve dusted with icing/confectioners' sugar. Best eaten the next day.

Sticky marzipan and cherry loaf

175 g/1½ sticks butter,
at room temperature

175 g/¾ cup caster/
granulated sugar

3 eggs

175 g/1 cup self-raising flour

85 g/scant 1 cup ground
almonds

175 g/6 oz. glacé cherries,
halved

75 g/2¾ oz. chilled marzipan,
finely grated

icing/confectioners' sugar,
for dusting

*a 900-g/2-lb loaf tin/pan,
greased and lined*

Serves 8–12

Studded with sweet glacé cherries and with a surprise layer of sticky marzipan running through the centre, this simple loaf cake will hit the spot.

Preheat the oven to 180°C (350°F) Gas 4. Put the butter and sugar in a large mixing bowl and beat until pale and creamy. Beat in the eggs one at a time. Sift the flour onto the mixture and then fold in. Stir in the cherries until evenly distributed in the mixture.

Spoon half the mixture into the prepared loaf tin/pan and level the surface. Sprinkle with the grated marzipan. Top with the remaining mixture and smooth the surface.

Bake for about 45 minutes, then remove the cake from the oven and cover the top with foil. Return it to the oven and bake for a further 25 minutes, until risen and golden and a skewer inserted in the centre of the cake comes out clean. Leave to cool in the tin/pan for about 10 minutes, then lift out on to a wire rack to cool. Serve the cake slightly warm or at room temperature.

100 g/¾ cup rolled oats

300 ml/1¼ cups hot milk

100 g/6½ tablespoons unsalted butter, at room temperature

60 g/5 tablespoons caster/granulated sugar

50 ml/3 tablespoons runny honey

1 teaspoon vanilla extract

1 egg, lightly beaten

1 teaspoon baking powder

120 g/1 cup plain/all-purpose flour

150 g/1 generous cup blueberries

150 g/1 generous cup raspberries

icing/confectioners' sugar, for dusting

a 900-g/2-lb loaf tin/pan, greased

Serves 6

Oatbake with blueberries and raspberries

This is the perfect dessert for a weekend brunch. The fresh berries make it irresistible and not too heavy. Serve it with a dollop of whipped cream or a drizzle of custard if you think it needs a little something else.

Preheat the oven to 180°C (350°F) Gas 4.

Put the oats and hot milk in a mixing bowl and set aside for a few minutes to allow the oats to absorb most of the milk and to cool down slightly.

Put the butter and sugar in a separate bowl and cream with a wooden spoon or handheld electric whisk until pale and fluffy. Stir in the honey and vanilla extract. Gradually add the egg, a little at a time, beating well after each addition.

Sift the baking powder and flour together, then fold into the butter mixture. Drain any remaining liquid from the oats, then stir into the mixing bowl.

Pour the mixture into the prepared loaf tin/pan and sprinkle the blueberries and raspberries evenly on top.

Bake in the preheated oven for 50–60 minutes, until a skewer inserted into the centre comes out clean. Leave to rest in the tin/pan for 10 minutes before turning out onto a wire rack to cool. Dust with a little icing/confectioners' sugar before serving.

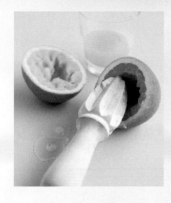

Marmalade and almond loaf

225 g/2 sticks butter, at room temperature

150 g/¾ cup golden caster/granulated sugar

freshly squeezed juice of ½ orange

finely grated zest of 1 orange

130 g/½ cup orange marmalade

4 large eggs

150 g/1 cup plus 2 tablespoons self-raising flour

75 g/½ cup ground almonds

a 900-g/2-lb loaf tin/pan, greased and base-lined with baking parchment

Serves 8–10

This is a moist cake streaked with zesty marmalade and kept a little squidgy by the addition of ground almonds. Be careful not to cook this in a very hot oven as the sugar content is high and the outside likes to brown. Serve it in chunky slices with Earl Grey tea.

Preheat the oven to 170°C (325°F) Gas 3.

Put the butter and sugar in a large mixing bowl and beat with an electric handheld whisk until the mixture is pale and light. Gradually add the orange juice, zest and the marmalade and swirl through with the whisk.

Lightly beat the eggs with a fork in a small bowl. Keep the electric whisk running in the creamed butter bowl and trickle the eggs in, 1 tablespoon at a time, beating thoroughly after each addition to stop them curdling. Finally, fold in the flour and ground almonds. Spoon the mixture into the prepared loaf tin/pan and bake on a low shelf in the preheated oven for about 45 minutes, until lightly golden on top. A skewer inserted in the middle should come out clean.

Leave the loaf to cool in the tin/pan for 15 minutes, then transfer to a wire rack to cool completely. It is easier to slice when it's cold – if you can resist its alluring aroma while it cools.

Lukullus

This is a German Christmas recipe which is very easy to make and incredibly 'moreish' to eat. A simple tiered stack of crunchy almond thins are layered with a rich dark chocolate paste. A perfect partner for a rich cup of coffee any time of year.

175 g/1½ sticks unsalted butter

100 g/¾ cup cocoa powder, plus extra to dust

150 g/¾ cup golden caster/ superfine sugar

1 egg

200 g/7 oz. almond thins, thin butter or langue de chat biscuits/ cookies

cocoa powder, to dust

icing/confectioners' sugar, to dust

a 450 g/1-lb. loaf tin/pan, lined with a single piece of foil or baking parchment

Serves 10–12

Melt the butter in a saucepan set over low heat. Once melted, sift in the cocoa powder and stir until smooth. Leave to cool for a few minutes.

Cream the sugar and egg together in a large bowl. Add the melted butter and cocoa mixture and mix to make a smooth chocolate paste.

To assemble the lukullus, start by spreading a thick layer of chocolate paste at the bottom of the prepared tin/pan, then add a layer of almond thins, then a thinner layer of paste. Repeat until all of the thins and chocolate paste have been used, finishing with a layer of chocolate paste. You should be able to make at least 7–8 almond layers. Put in the fridge and leave to chill for at least 1 hour.

Carefully invert the loaf tin/pan and turn the lukullus out onto a serving plate. Remove the foil and dust the top with cocoa powder and icing/ confectioners' sugar.

To serve, use a serrated knife to cut into thin slices.

This is best eaten on the day it is made as it contains raw egg, but if you don't manage to eat it all at once, store in an airtight container in the fridge.

Tarts, Pies and Cheesecakes

375 g/13 oz. ready-rolled sweet shortcrust pastry

18 pecan halves, to decorate

Date filling

60 g/2 oz. Medjool dates, pitted

30 ml/2 tablespoons double/heavy cream

1 tablespoon water

30 g/2 tablespoons unsalted butter, melted

30 g/2 tablespoons light brown soft sugar

1 egg

a few drops of vanilla extract

55 g/½ cup plain/all-purpose flour

1 teaspoon baking powder

Pecan bourbon filling

1 tablespoon bourbon whiskey

40 g/3 tablespoons soft light brown sugar

55 ml/¾ cup golden/corn syrup

1 egg, beaten

20 g/1½ tablespoons unsalted butter, melted

60 g/½ cup pecan nuts, chopped

6 x 9-cm/3½-inch loose-based fluted tartlet tins/pans, greased

Makes 6 tartlets

Pecan and bourbon tartlets

Nutty, with the subtle flavour of bourbon coming through, these smart, irresistible little tarts are perfect for winter entertaining. Bake a batch at Christmastime to round off a festive feast.

Preheat the oven to 180°C (350°F) Gas 4.

Line the tartlet tins/pans with the sweet shortcrust pastry and trim the excess dough neatly around the edges. Refrigerate while you make the filling.

To make date filling, blitz the dates to a paste in a food processor or simply chop them very finely. Mix with the cream and water and set aside.

Put the butter and sugar in a mixing bowl and mix well, then add the egg, vanilla, flour and baking powder. Finally, add date mixture and fold in well.

Remove the chilled tartlet shells from the fridge and spoon about 1½ tablespoons of the date sponge into them. Bake in the preheated oven for 15 minutes, then remove from the oven (leaving the oven on).

In the meantime, make the pecan bourbon filling. Put the bourbon, sugar and syrup in a mixing bowl and mix well. Add the egg, mix well, then stir in the melted butter and pecan nuts.

Spoon the pecan bourbon filling on top of the tartlets and spread evenly. Decorate with 3 pecan halves and return to the oven for another 10 minutes. Remove from the oven and leave to cool before serving.

500 g/1 lb. 2 oz. ready-made shortcrust pastry

1.3 kg/3 lbs. tart eating apples, such as Cox's or Jonagold

100 g/½ cup sugar

100 g/¾ cup sultanas/golden raisins

1 teaspoon ground cinnamon

1 tablespoon freshly squeezed lemon juice

whipped cream, to serve

Streusel topping

90 g/½ cup light brown soft sugar

45 g/½ cup plus 2 tablespoons plain/all-purpose flour

120 g/1 stick unsalted butter, chilled

1 teaspoon each cinnamon, nutmeg and allspice

a pinch of fine sea salt

80 g/½ cup walnuts, chopped

a 24-cm/9½-inch springform cake tin/pan, buttered and floured

Serves 6–8

Dutch apple pie

There are several different ways to top this alternative to a classic American apple pie, including a lattice crust or this streusel topping, which is not strictly speaking Dutch as it comes from the Amish communities of America.

Preheat the oven to 180°C (350°F) Gas 4.

Roll out the pastry on a floured work surface and line the tin/pan with the pastry, all the way up the sides to the top edge. Refrigerate while you prepare the apples.

Peel, core and dice the apples and put them in a bowl. Add the sugar, sultanas/golden raisins, cinnamon and lemon juice and mix well using your hands.

In a food processor, combine all the topping ingredients, except the walnuts, and process to form coarse crumbs. Add the walnuts and pulse just a few times to combine.

Put the apple mixture in the pastry-lined tin/pan. Sprinkle the streusel topping over the top in an even layer, going all the way to the edges and tidy up the edges of the pastry.

Cover with foil and bake in the preheated oven for about 30 minutes. Remove the foil and continue baking until the top of the pie is golden, about 25–30 minutes.

Remove from the oven and let cool. Serve warm with whipped cream.

Pumpkin pie

375 g/13 oz. ready-rolled sweet shortcrust pastry

1–2 tablespoons milk

425-g/14-oz. can puréed pumpkin

2 eggs

1 egg yolk

150 g/¾ cup light brown soft sugar

½ teaspoon ground ginger

1 teaspoon ground cinnamon

a pinch of grated nutmeg

a pinch of ground cloves

a pinch of salt

125 ml/½ cup double/heavy cream

2–3 teaspoons caster/granulated sugar

icing/confectioners' sugar, for dusting

a 23-cm/9-inch round pie dish

a small star-shaped cutter

Serves 6

A classic American holiday recipe that can be whipped up in no time and that showcases the humble pumpkin at its sweetest and best.

Preheat the oven to 180°C (350°F) Gas 4 and place a baking sheet on the middle shelf to preheat.

Sprinkle a little flour on a clean work surface. Roll out the dough until it's big enough to fit your pie dish. Carefully lift up the pastry (it may help to lift it while on the rolling pin) and lay it in the pie dish. Trim any excess pastry from around the edge with a small knife.

Gather up any scraps of dough, knead very lightly to bring together into a ball and roll out again. Use the star-shaped cutter to stamp out lots of stars. Brush the edges of the pie with a little milk and stick the pastry stars, slightly overlapping, all around the edge.

Chill the pastry case in the fridge while you prepare the filling.

Put the puréed pumpkin, whole eggs and yolk, brown sugar, ginger, cinnamon, nutmeg, cloves, salt and cream in a large bowl and whisk until well mixed and smooth.

Carefully pour the mixture into the pie dish, brush the stars with a little more milk and scatter the caster/granulated sugar over them.

Put the pie on the hot baking sheet in the preheated oven. Bake for about 35 minutes, or until the filling has set and the pastry is golden.

Remove the pie from the oven. Leave to cool to room temperature before dusting with icing/confectioners' sugar.

Crust

60 g/4 tablespoons unsalted butter

125 g/4½ oz. plain digestive or wheaten biscuits

1 tablespoon caster/granulated sugar

Filling

500 g/1 lb. ricotta cheese

250 ml/1 cup sour cream

2 large free-range eggs

100 g/¾ cup icing/confectioners' sugar

2 tablespoons ground almonds

grated zest and freshly squeezed juice of 2 lemons

Topping

2 tablespoons flaked/slivered almonds

fresh summer berries

a 23-cm/9-inch springform cake tin/pan, buttered

Serves 8

Lemon ricotta cheesecake with summer berries

This is a light, baked cheesecake with lots of fresh raspberries, strawberries and blueberries so it makes a lovely summer dessert. Ricotta is a low-fat soft Italian cheese usually sold in tubs.

Preheat the oven to 150°C (300°F) Gas 2.

To make the base, melt the butter in a small saucepan set over low heat. Crush the biscuits in a food processor or put them in a plastic bag and crush finely with a rolling pin. Tip the crumbs into a mixing bowl and add the melted butter and the sugar. Mix well with a wooden spoon then tip the mixture into the tin/pan. Roughly spread the crumbs in the tin/pan so they are evenly distributed then, using the back of a metal spoon, press the crumbs onto the base of the tin/pan to make an even layer. Put the tin/pan in the fridge to chill while you make the filling.

Put the ricotta and sour cream into a large mixing bowl. Break the eggs into the bowl, then add the icing/confectioner's sugar, ground almonds and lemon zest and juice and beat together.

Pour the filling carefully into the tin/pan then scatter the flaked almonds on the top. Bake in the preheated oven for 1¼ hours then turn off the oven and leave the cheesecake inside (don't open the door) to cool slowly as the oven cools down. After 1½ hours, remove the cheesecake from the oven and gently remove it from the tin/pan.

Store your cheesecake in an airtight container in the fridge and eat it within 3 days. For the best flavour, remove it from the fridge about 30 minutes before eating. Serve the cheesecake either topped with or surrounded by the berries or put them in a separate bowl so everyone can help themselves.

450 g/1 lb. ready-rolled sweet
shortcrust pastry

Filling

2 large eggs

275 ml/1¼ cups maple syrup

150 ml/⅔ cup double/
heavy cream

2 tablespoons plain/
all-purpose flour

100 g/1 cup walnut pieces

icing/confectioners' sugar or
maple sugar, for sprinkling

a 23-cm/9-inch deep pie dish

baking beans

maple leaf pastry cutters

Serves 8

Maple pie

*This wonderful, sweet maple pie is guaranteed to be a hit. If you can
find cookie cutters in the shape of maple leaves, they make the perfect
decoration for the top.*

Sprinkle a little flour on a clean work surface. Roll out the dough and use it to
line your pie dish, smoothing it out so there are no bubbles of air. Roll the pin
over the top of the pie dish to cut off the overhanging dough, saving the pastry
for the decorations. Gently use your thumbs to press the pastry sides upwards
so the pastry stands about 5 mm/½ inch higher than the rim of the dish. Prick
the base a few times with a fork, then chill in the fridge for 20 minutes.

Preheat the oven to 200°C (400°F) Gas 6.

Take the chilled pastry out of the fridge. Cut a round of baking parchment
36 cm/14 inches across. Crumple the paper to make it soft then open it out and
gently press it into the pastry case to cover the base and sides. Fill the case with
baking beans and bake in the preheated oven for 15 minutes then carefully
remove the paper and beans. Turn the oven down to 190°C (375°F) Gas 5 and
bake the pastry for 5 minutes more, until a light gold colour. Put a baking sheet
into the oven to heat up.

To make the filling break the eggs into a mixing bowl. Add the maple syrup,
cream and flour and mix well with a rotary whisk until smooth.

Remove the pastry case from the oven. Stand the pie dish on the hot baking
sheet and scatter the walnuts over the base of the pastry case. Pour the filling
over the nuts then bake for 30 minutes, until lightly coloured.

Roll out the leftover pastry fairly thinly and cut into shapes using fancy cutters
(maple leaves or whatever you like). Remove the pie from the oven and gently
arrange the pastry shapes on top. Return the pie to the oven and bake for
10 minutes more. Carefully remove it from the oven and leave to cool. Eat while
still warm. Sprinkle with icing/confectioners' or maple sugar before serving.

Marbled chocolate cheesecake

Chocolate crumb base

175 g/6 oz. chocolate-coated digestives, chocolate chip cookies or graham crackers

75 g/5 tablespoons unsalted butter

25 g/2 tablespoons light brown soft sugar

Marbled chocolate filling

150 g/5 oz. dark/bittersweet chocolate, chopped

750 g/1 lb. 10 oz. full-fat cream cheese, at room temperature

250 g/1¼ cups golden caster/granulated sugar

1 teaspoon vanilla extract

2 large eggs

a 23-cm/9-inch springform cake tin/pan, greased and lined with baking parchment

Serves 8

This decadent dessert would make a wonderfully indulgent birthday cake, adorned with golden candles.

Preheat the oven to 180°C (350°F) Gas 4.

To make the chocolate crumb base, crush the cookies in a food processor or put them in a plastic bag and crush finely with a rolling pin. Melt the butter and sugar in a small pan over gentle heat, then stir in the cookie crumbs. Press the mixture evenly over the base of the prepared cake tin/pan. Bake for 15 minutes, then remove from the oven, lightly press the cookie base down again and leave to cool completely. Reduce the oven temperature to 160°C (325°F) Gas 3.

Melt the chocolate and 50 ml/3 tablespoons water in a small bowl set over a saucepan of barely simmering water, then keep it warm.

Put the cream cheese and sugar in a large bowl. Using a wooden spoon or electric whisk, beat until soft and creamy. Put the eggs and vanilla extract in a separate bowl and whisk well. Gradually beat the eggs into the cheese mixture. Pour approximately 250 ml/1 cup of the mixture into a jug/pitcher, then pour the remaining mixture into the cake tin/pan.

Stir the warm chocolate into the reserved cheese mixture. Pour the chocolate mixture in a wide zigzag pattern over the surface of the cheesecake, edge to edge. Draw the handle of a thick wooden spoon through the pattern, zig-zagging in the opposite direction so the mixtures give a marbled effect. Do not overwork or the pattern will be lost. Keep it simple and the edges neat.

Bake in the preheated oven for 20–25 minutes, or until the cheesecake starts to puff slightly around the edges but is still very soft in the centre. Transfer the tin/pan to a wire rack and loosen the edges of the cheesecake with a thin-bladed knife. When completely cold, refrigerate for at least 3 hours before removing from the tin/pan.

Pear, almond and mascarpone tart

4 very ripe pears

1 tablespoon freshly squeezed lemon juice

6 tablespoons caster/granulated sugar

125 g/½ cup mascarpone

1 egg

1 tablespoon plain/all-purpose flour

100 g/⅔ cup flaked/slivered almonds

chilled cream or vanilla ice cream, to serve

Pastry

200 g/1½ cups plain/all-purpose flour

4 tablespoons caster/granulated sugar

80 g/5½ tablespoons unsalted butter, chilled and cubed

a 24-cm/10-inch loose-bottomed tart tin/pan, lightly greased and floured

Serves 8

Sweet, nutty and creamy, this recipe works best if the pears are on the overripe side so that they are fork-tender when cooked.

To make the pastry, put the flour and sugar in a food processor and pulse to combine. With the motor running, add the butter and 1–2 tablespoons cold water and mix until the mixture resembles coarse breadcrumbs and starts to gather in lumps. Transfer to a lightly-floured work surface and briefly knead to form a ball. Wrap in clingfilm/plastic wrap and chill for 1 hour, until firm.

Preheat the oven to 180°C (350°F) Gas 4.

Coarsely grate the chilled pastry into a large bowl. Using lightly floured hands, scatter the grated pastry into the prepared tart tin/pan and use your fingers to gently press it in until the entire base and the side of the tin/pan are covered. Bake in the preheated oven for about 25 minutes, until lightly golden. Let cool.

Peel, halve and core the pears. Put them in a non-metal bowl with the lemon juice and 1 tablespoon of the sugar. Put the remaining sugar in a food processor. Add the mascarpone, egg and flour and process to form a thick paste. Spread the mixture over the pastry. Arrange the pears on top and scatter with the almonds and sugar. Bake in the still-hot oven for 40–45 minutes, until the pears are soft and the mascarpone mixture has set. Serve in slices with cream or vanilla ice cream on the side.

Baked cheesecake

Who doesn't love a good baked cheesecake? Make this the day before you want to serve it and don't stress about cracks in the surface – they add character! For the best result, bring the cream cheese, eggs and sour cream to room temperature before using.

160 g/6 oz. very dry, slightly sweet biscuits, such as Rich Tea or graham crackers or Arnott's Coffee Biscuits

225 g/1 cup plus 2 tablespoons caster/superfine sugar

100 g/7 tablespoons unsalted butter

750 g/1 lb. 10 oz. full-fat cream cheese

5 eggs

300 ml/1¼ cups sour cream

1 teaspoon finely grated lemon zest

a 23-cm/9-inch springform cake tin/pan, base-lined with baking parchment and lightly greased

Serves 8–10

Preheat the oven to 170°C (325°F) Gas 3. Wrap the entire outside of the prepared cake tin/pan in 2 layers of foil.

Put the biscuits/crackers and 1 tablespoon of the sugar in a food processor and process to a fine crumb. Add the melted butter and process until well combined. Tip the crumb mixture into the prepared tin/pan and spread evenly over the base. Use the bottom of a glass tumbler to firmly press the crumb mixture into the tin/pan. Bake in the preheated oven for 20 minutes. Remove and let cool completely.

Put the cream cheese and remaining sugar in a bowl, preferably that of an electric mixer with a paddle attachment, and beat for 2 minutes, until smooth and well combined. Add the eggs, one at a time, beating well between each addition and scraping down the side of the mixer bowl. Add the lemon zest and sour cream. Beat until the mixture is lump-free.

Pour the mixture into the prepared tin/pan and level the top with a pallette knife. Bake in the still-hot oven for 1 hour, until the top of the cheesecake is golden but the centre is still wobbly. Turn the oven off and partially open the oven door. Let the cheesecake cool in the oven for 1 hour. Refrigerate for 6 hours, or ideally overnight.

Remove the cheesecake from the refrigerator 1 hour before eating. When ready to serve, run a warm, dry knife around the edge of the cake and remove the springform side. Cut into generous wedges.

1 recipe Chocolate Dough
(see page 230)

1 large pear, peeled, halved
and cored

20 g/3 tablespoons shelled
hazelnuts, roughly chopped

2 tablespoons apricot jam
(optional)

Biscuit dough

45 g/3 tablespoons unsalted
butter

100 g/scant ½ cup of
caster/granulated sugar

1 egg

1 teaspoon baking powder

100 g/¾ cup plain/
all-purpose flour

Chocolate
hazelnut cream

90 g/3 oz. dark/bittersweet
chocolate, finely chopped

90 g/3 oz. milk chocolate,
finely chopped

180 ml/¾ cup single/
light cream

40 g/6 tablespoons shelled
hazelnuts, roughly chopped

*a 23-cm/9-inch loose-based
fluted tart tin/pan, greased*

Serves 8–12 slices

Chocolate, pear and hazelnut tart

This stunning dessert is fit for your most discerning dinner guests, but it is also simple enough to make for a sophisticated picnic.

Preheat the oven to 170°C (325°F) Gas 3.

Line the tart tin/pan with the dough and trim the excess dough neatly around the edges. Refrigerate while you make the biscuit dough.

Put the butter and sugar in a mixing bowl and mix with an electric whisk to combine. Mix in the egg and baking powder with the whisk, then gently fold in the flour by hand until evenly combined.

To make the chocolate hazelnut cream, lightly toast the hazelnuts in a dry frying pan. Put the chocolate in a mixing bowl. Put the cream in a saucepan and gently bring to the boil over low heat, stirring frequently. Pour into the mixing bowl and whisk until you get a smooth cream, then stir in the hazelnuts. Gently fold the biscuit dough into the chocolate hazelnut mixture and mix well. Remove the tart shell from the fridge and pour in the chocolate hazelnut cream.

Cut the pear into about 12 slim wedges and arrange in a circle on top of the tart filling. Sprinkle the hazelnuts over the top. Bake in the preheated oven for about 25 minutes.

Put the apricot jam, if using, in a small saucepan and heat gently until melted and runny. Brush the jam roughly over the tart (avoiding the hazelnuts) with a pastry brush and leave for a few more minutes before serving.

450 g/1 lb. ready-rolled sweet shortcrust pastry

Lime filling

5 eggs, separated

1 x 400-g/14-oz. can sweetened condensed milk

2 tablespoons grated lime zest

150 ml/½ cup plus 1 tablespoon freshly squeezed lime juice (about 5–6 limes)

¼ teaspoon cream of tartar

Cream topping

250 ml/1 cup whipping cream

3 tablepoons vanilla sugar

zest of 1 large lime, pared into fine shreds

a 23-cm/10-inch tart tin/pan

Serves 6–8

Key lime pie

The name of this pie comes from the Florida Keys where once, until a hurricane destroyed many of the orchards, limes were grown plentifully. The sharp lime juice counters the intense sweetness of the condensed milk, yielding a tangy but deeply satisfying creamy filling.

Preheat the oven to 190°C (375°F) Gas 5.

Roll out the pastry and use to line the tart tin/pan. Cover the edge of the tart with thin strips of foil. Prick the base all over with a fork and leave to chill for 30–40 minutes. Bake in the preheated oven for 8–10 minutes. Remove the foil strips and brush the inside of the pastry case with beaten egg white. Return to the oven for another 8–10 minutes. Let the pastry cool in the tin/pan.

To make the lime filling, put 1 whole egg and 3 egg yolks in a bowl and beat until blended. Whisk in the condensed milk and lime zest. Gradually whisk in the lime juice.

Put the egg whites and cream of tartar in a separate, grease-free bowl and whisk until stiff but not dry. Beat 2 tablespoons of the egg white mixture into the egg yolk mixture, then fold in the remainder with a spatula. Scrape into the pastry case and bake in a preheated oven at 180°C (350°F) Gas 4 for about 20 minutes or until risen and just firm in the centre. Remove from the oven and let cool in its tin/pan on a wire rack. It will deflate as it cools.

When cool, make the topping. Put the cream and 2 tablespoons of the sugar in a bowl, whip until softly stiff, then spread over the lime filling. Toss the shreds of lime zest in the remaining sugar and use to decorate the tart. Serve cold but not chilled.

1 tablespoon cornflour/cornstarch

60 g/scant ⅓ cup
caster/granulated sugar

1 egg plus 1 egg yolk

100 ml/⅓ cup milk

150 ml/⅔ cup double/heavy cream

1 vanilla pod, split lengthwise

300 g/1½ cups strawberries,
hulled and halved

5 tablespoons apricot preserve

freshly squeezed juice of 2 lemons

Pastry

250 g/2 scant cups plain/
all-purpose baking flour

50 g/½ cup plus 3 tablespoons
ground almonds

100 g/7 tablespoons butter, chilled

100 g/½ cup cream cheese

50 g/¼ cup caster/
granulated sugar

1 egg yolk

1 teaspoon vanilla extract

grated zest of 1 lemon

an 8-cm/3-inch cookie cutter

*2 x 12-hole tartlet tins/pans,
greased*

baking beans

*a piping bag, fitted with a large
round nozzle/tip*

Makes 24 tartlets

Strawberry tartlets

*These dainty tartlets are the height of sophistication. They are the perfect
accompaniment to a glass of chilled champagne at a summer party.*

To make the pastry, sift the flour into a mixing bowl and stir in the almonds.
Rub in the butter until the mixture resembles fine breadcrumbs. Add the cream
cheese, sugar, egg yolk, vanilla extract and lemon zest and mix to a soft dough
with your fingers. Wrap in clingfilm/plastic wrap and chill for 1 hour.

Preheat the oven to 180°C (350°F) Gas 4. Roll out the pastry to a thickness of
3 mm/⅛ inch. Stamp out 24 rounds with the cutter and press one into each hole
of the prepared tin/pan. Line the pastry cases with baking parchment, fill with
baking beans and bake in the preheated oven for 12–15 minutes, until golden
brown and crisp. Let cool on a wire rack.

To make the crème pâtissèrie, put the cornflour/cornstarch, sugar, egg and egg
yolk in a bowl and whisk until creamy. Put the milk, cream and vanilla pod
in a saucepan and bring to the boil. Pour the hot milk over the egg mixture,
whisking continuously. Return to the pan and cook for about 2 minutes, until
thick. Remove the vanilla pod, pass the mixture through a sieve/strainer and let
cool. Spoon the cooled crème pâtissière into the piping bag and fill the pastry
cases. Arrange some strawberry halves on top. Put the preserve and
lemon juice in a saucepan and heat until runny, pass
through a sieve/strainer, let cool slightly, then
brush over the top of each tartlet to glaze
using a pastry brush.

Rustic plum tart

This recipe was created with late summer in mind. It's very simple, light and fruity, and really you can make it with any ripe fruit you have a glut of. A variation that works particularly well, though, is apple and cinnamon, which is the winter partner to the summer plum.

90 g/½ cup golden caster/granulated sugar

1 egg

40 ml/2½ cups groundnut/peanut or vegetable oil

55 ml/¼ cup whole milk

140 g/1 cup plus 1 tablespoon plain/all-purpose flour

1 teaspoon baking powder

a few drops of vanilla extract

6 large plums, pitted and halved

2 tablespoons apricot jam, to glaze (optional)

a 20-cm/8-inch springform tin/pan, lined with baking parchment

Serves 6–8

Preheat the oven 180°C (350°F) Gas 4.

Put the sugar and egg in a mixing bowl and mix with an electric whisk. Add the oil, milk, flour, baking powder and vanilla and mix again until combined. Transfer to the prepared baking tin/pan and spread evenly. Sit the plums, cut side up, over the mixture.

Bake in the preheated oven for about 30 minutes, or until deep golden. Remove from the oven and leave to cool for a few minutes.

In the meantime, put the apricot jam, if using, in a small saucepan and heat gently until melted and runny. Brush the jam all over the tart with a pastry brush and leave for a few more minutes before serving.

Substitute ½ teaspoon ground cinnamon for the vanilla extract, and 1 Bramley or Golden Delicious apple, cored and sliced, for the plums if you want to try the winter version.

Spiced pumpkin cheesecakes with nutmeg icing

Cheesecakes

75 g/5 tablespoons butter

125 g/4 oz. shortcake or shortbread biscuits or graham crackers, broken into pieces

200 g/6½ oz. cream cheese

100 g/½ cup soft curd cheese

100 g/½ cup canned pumpkin purée

100 g/½ cup caster/granulated sugar

2 medium eggs, lightly beaten

2 pinches each of ground cloves, ginger, allspice and nutmeg

orange sanding sugar, to decorate (optional)

Nutmeg icing

50 g/¼ cup caster/granulated sugar

100 g/3½ cup oz. cream cheese

½ teaspoon freshly grated nutmeg

a 12-hole muffin tin/pan, lined with paper cases

Makes 12 cakes

Have fun with these for Halloween – use themed cupcake cases and decorate with sugarcraft sprinkles.

Preheat the oven to 150°C (300°F) Gas 3.

First make the base for the cheesecakes. Melt the butter in a small saucepan and leave to cool slightly.

Grind the biscuits/crackers to crumbs in a food processor. Add all but 1 tablespoon of the melted butter (reserve this for the icing) and whizz to combine. Divide between the cupcake cases and press down firmly with the back of a teaspoon.

Put the cream cheese, curd cheese, pumpkin purée, sugar, beaten eggs and spices in an electric mixer (or use a large mixing bowl and an electric whisk). Whisk until smooth and combined. Tip the mixture into a jug/pitcher, then pour it into the cupcake cases, dividing it equally.

Bake the cakes in the preheated oven for 15 minutes. Leave to cool completely – they will set as they cool.

To make the nutmeg icing, whisk the ingredients together (including the reserved butter) and put a spoonful on each cheesecake. If you are not eating them immediately, refrigerate them but let them come to room temperature before eating. Sprinkle with sanding sugar, if you like. They are soft-set, so they are best eaten with teaspoons.

Chocolate dough

125 g/1 cup plain/all-purpose flour

3 tablespoons unsweetened cocoa powder

115g/1 stick unsalted butter

5 tablespoons caster/granulated sugar

1 egg

Chocolate filling

70 g/½ cup golden caster/granulated sugar

1 egg

55 g/½ cup plain/all-purpose flour

½ teaspoon baking powder

2 teaspoons cocoa powder

10 g/1 tablespoon unsalted butter

35 g/1 oz. dark/bittersweet chocolate, chopped

Chocolate ganache

50 g/1½ oz. dark/bittersweet chocolate, finely chopped

50 g/1½ oz. milk chocolate, finely chopped

150 ml/⅔ cup double/heavy cream

a handful of shelled pistachio nuts, chopped, to decorate

6 x 9-cm/3½-inch loose-based fluted tartlet tins/pans, greased

Makes 6 tartlets

Chocolate and pistachio tartlets

These stunning little tartlets light up any table. There is something incredibly satisfying about smothering them in the rich ganache, and they are even more satisfying to eat.

Preheat the oven to 180°C (350°F) Gas 4.

To make the chocolate dough, put the flour, cocoa, butter and sugar in a food processor and blitz until you get crumbs. Add the egg and mix again. Take the dough out of the processor and bring together into a ball. Roll and line the tartlet tins/pans and trim the excess dough neatly around the edges. Refrigerate while you make the filling.

To make the chocolate filling, put the sugar and egg in a mixing bowl and beat with an electric whisk until pale yellow. Gently fold in the flour, baking powder and cocoa powder. In a heatproof bowl, melt the butter and chocolate over a pan of simmering water, then add to the mixing bowl. Add 2 tablespoons water and mix well.

Spoon about 1½ tablespoons chocolate filling into each tartlet. Bake in the preheated oven for 15 minutes. Remove from the oven and leave to cool for 10 minutes.

To make the ganache, put the chocolate in a mixing bowl. Put the cream in a saucepan and gently bring to the boil over low heat, stirring frequently. Pour into the mixing bowl and whisk until you get a smooth cream.

Pour the chocolate ganache into the tartlets, then scatter the pistachio nuts over the top. Refrigerate and serve chilled.

Rhubarb meringue pie

The soft, snowy peaks sit beautifully on this tangy pie. Dive in!

100 g/6½ tablespoons unsalted butter, at room temperature

65 g/½ cup caster/granulated sugar

2 eggs, separated

90 g/¾ cup plain/all-purpose flour

1 teaspoon baking powder

50 ml/3 tablespoons milk

Rhubarb filling

3–4 sticks of rhubarb, trimmed and roughly chopped

1 teaspoon ground cinnamon

65 g/⅓ cup plus 2 teaspoons caster/granulated sugar

1 teaspoon vanilla extract

50 g/½ cup flaked/slivered almonds

a 24-cm/10-inch loose-bottomed, fluted tart tin/pan, greased

Serves 6–8

Preheat the oven to 180°C (350°F) Gas 4.

Cream the butter and sugar until pale and fluffy. Add the egg yolks one by one, mixing well. Mix the flour and baking powder together, then add half to the butter mixture, mixing well. Add half the milk and mix well. Finally, add the remaining flour mixture, mix, then add the remaining milk and mix well. Transfer the dough to the tart tin/pan and push and press it until the base and sides are evenly covered with a layer of dough.

To make the filling, mix the rhubarb, cinnamon and 2 teaspoons of the sugar together, then spread roughly over the tart.

Whisk the egg whites until they hold soft peaks, then gradually add the remaining sugar, whisking until firm. Fold in the vanilla extract. Spoon on top of the pie, making peaks as you go, and scatter the almonds over the top. Bake in the preheated oven for 35–40 minutes.

The appeal of this fruit tart is its rustic, homemade charm. This is nothing like a tart from a fancy patisserie! Use slightly underripe peaches. You can add nuts and raisins and a little cinnamon when you mix in the sugar.

Free-form peach pie

First make the pastry using the food processor: put the flour, salt, cinnamon and sugar into the bowl of the processor. Run the machine for a few seconds just to combine all the ingredients. Cut the butter into small pieces and add to the bowl of the processor and blitz until the ingredients look like coarse crumbs. Pour in 3 tablespoons cold water through the feed tube and run the machine until the dough comes together in a ball.

Sprinkle a little flour over your work surface and gently knead and work the dough for a few seconds until it looks smooth. Put the sheet of non-stick baking parchment onto the work surface. Put the ball of dough in the middle of the paper. Sprinkle a rolling pin with flour and gently roll out the dough to a circle about 30 cm/12 inches across. Slide the sheet of paper with the dough on it onto the baking sheet and chill in the fridge for 15 minutes while you make the filling.

Preheat the oven to 200°C (400°F) Gas 6.

Sprinkle the sliced peaches with the 3 tablespoons sugar, and mix gently. Remove the dough from the fridge. Heap the sliced fruit into the centre of the dough, mounding it evenly. Leave a wide border of pastry, about 9 cm/ 3½ inches, without fruit. Gently fold the border of pastry over the fruit so the fruit in the centre is uncovered, leaving a gap of about 2.5 cm/1 inch between the fruit and the fold, and gently pinch the folds or pleats of pastry together every 6 cm/2½ inches. Try not to press the dough down onto the fruit.

Lightly brush the pastry with cold water then sprinkle with caster sugar. Bake in the preheated oven for 40 minutes, until golden brown. Remove it from the oven and leave to cool on its sheet for 10 minutes. Slide the tart off its paper lining and onto a serving platter while it is still warm, and serve.

For the pastry

225 g/1⅔ cups plain/
all-purpose flour

a pinch of salt

a pinch of ground cinnamon

2 tablespoons caster/
granulated sugar

150 g/1¼ sticks unsalted butter,
chilled

For the filling

750 g/1 lb. 10 oz. peaches
(about 5 medium peaches),
pitted and sliced

3 tablespoons caster/granulated
sugar, plus extra for sprinkling

Serves 6

Index

Recipe credits

Susannah Blake
Angel food cake
Apple and sultana scones
Carrot and cardamom
  cupcakes
Coffee and walnut cake
Hazelnut tea cookies
Honey buns
Lavender cupcakes
Maple and pecan cupcakes
Passion fruit butterfly cakes
Russian poppy seed cake
Spiced carrot and pistachio
  cake
Sticky marzipan and cherry
  loaf
Toasted teacakes
Victoria sandwich cake

Claire Burnet
Devilishly delicious
  chocolate cake
Ginger marble cake bars
Lukullus
Triple chocolate cupside-
  down cakes
White chocolate and fresh
  raspberry cookies

Maxine Clark
Chocolate, cherry and
  macadamia teabreads
Double chocolate chip
  cookies
Marbled chocolate
  cheesecake
Queen of Sheba chocolate
  and almond cake
Warm chocolate muffins

Linda Collister
Blueberry lemon pound cake
Cherry berry buns
Festive fruit and nut pound
  cake
Free-form peach pie
Fresh orange cake
Lemon ricotta cheesecake
  with summer berries
Little peanut butter cakes
Maple pie

Ross Dobson
Baked cheesecake
Easy banana bread
Little almond, polenta and
  lemon syrup cakes
Pear, almond and
  mascarpone tart
Spiced oatmeal cake with
  chocolate and cinnamon
  frosting

Tonia George
Exploding berry crumble
  muffins
Marmalade and almond loaf
Sugary jam doughnut muffins

Brian Glover
Courgette, lemon and
  poppyseed cake with
  lemon butter frosting
Key lime pie

Hannah Miles
Apple and orange
  gingerbread
Chocolate and cherry pies
Coconut and pumpkin
  power bars
Cranberry and white
  chocolate cupcakes
Pear and blackberry scone
  round
Rose and violet cream pies
Strawberry tartlets
Walnut and cinnamon
  macarons

Miisa Mink
Birthday cake with cream
  and berries
Oatbake with blueberries
  and raspberries
Rhubarb meringue pie

Isidora Popovic
Chocolate, pear and hazelnut
  tart
Chocolate and pistachio
  tartlets
Cranberry, orange and

pistachio muffins
Cranberry, sherry and vine
  fruit cake
Easter egg biscuits
Ginger and chilli caramel
  cookies
Granola bars
Fig, apricot and nut biscotti
Florentines
Lemon loaf with white
  chocolate frosting
Pecan and bourbon tartlets
Rustic plum tart
Stollen
Wholemeal spelt, carrot,
  apple and pumpkin seed
  muffins

Sarah Randell
Apple and amaretto cake
Banana and passion-fruit loaf
Blackcurrant, berry and
  hazelnut crumble cake
Chocolate fudge raspberry
  shortbread bars
Cinnamon blueberry cake
Coconut, apricot and lime
  slices
Crunchy prune and vanilla
  custard brioche cakes
Hazelnut cheesecake bars
Honey, toasted pine nut and
  pumpkin-seed flapjacks
Lemon squares
Lime drizzle cake with
  coconut frosting
Mocha swirl loaf with
  espresso icing
Mulled wine and cranberry
  tea bread
Passion-fruit sandwiches
Scones with strawberry jam
  and plenty of clotted cream
Spiced pumpkin cheesecakes
  with nutmeg icing
St. Clement's macarons
Toffee pear muffins
Tropical chai pineapple cake

Annie Rigg
Butterscotch brownies
Cinnamon sticky buns
Deep dark chocolate

brownies
Easy fruit cake
Gingerbread brownies
High summer cake
Pain d'épices
Peanut butter and jam
  brownies
Pumpkin pie
Ricciarelli
Rocky roadies
Shortbread
Sugared refrigerator cookies

Laura Washburn
Apple and carrot bread with
  walnuts
Apple, fig and nut bars
Apple spice muffins
Applesauce cookies
Dutch apple pie
Pear and chocolate muffins

Photography credits

Steve Baxter
Page 199 background

Martin Brigdale
Pages 21–22, 25–26, 42, 47, 52,
  55, 60, 124, 126a, 127, 132,
  152, 186, 194

Peter Cassidy
Pages 1, 10, 16a, 17–19, 24,
  29–31, 36–37, 49a, 54, 63–64,
  68–72, 80–81, 84–85, 114–117,
  140, 143, 147, 155, 163, 167,
  172, 174, 176, 188–190, 191a,
  192, 197, 204–207, 215, 218
  background, 220, 221a, 226a,
  227, 231–232, 233a

Laura Edwards
Pages 4–5, 87–88, 89
  background, 91, 96–99,
  102–103, 105, 133

Tara Fisher
Page 66a

Jonathan Gregson
Pages 8, 11, 14, 20, 34, 40–41,
  58–59, 89a,108, 166, 171, 198,
  199a, 200–201

Richard Jung
Pages 110, 157a, 175a, 223

Lisa Linder
Pages 51, 118a, 119–120, 121a,
  148, 149a, 151, 181, 208

William Lingwood
Pages 35, 50, 82a, 150, 187,
  196

Diana Miller
Pages 185, 193

Steve Painter
Pages 61, 86, 94, 160, 168

William Reavell
Pages 6 below left, 15, 16
  background, 27, 32–33,
  46, 49 background, 53,
  77, 90, 106–107, 109a,
  121 background, 122
  background, 125, 128–131,
  138, 141, 154, 164–165,
  202, 210, 224–225, 230

Kate Whitaker
Pages 2, 6 all apart from
  below left, 12–13, 23, 28,
  39 background, 44–45,
  48, 56–57, 62, 65, 66
  background, 67, 73–76, 78,
  82 background, 83, 92–93,
  95, 100–101, 104, 109
  background, 112–113,
  118 background, 126
  background, 134–137, 142,
  144–146, 149 background,
  153, 156, 157 background,
  158–159, 161–162, 169–170,
  175 background, 177–180,
  183 background, 184, 191
  background, 195, 209, 213